PSYCHODYNAMICS: THE SCIENCE OF UNCONSCIOUS MENTAL FORCES

PSYCHODYNAMICS: THE SCIENCE OF UNCONSCIOUS MENTAL FORCES

GERALD S. BLUM

The University of Michigan

WADSWORTH PUBLISHING COMPANY, INC., BELMONT, CALIFORNIA

L. C. cat. card No.: 66-12644

Printed in the United States of America

SERIES FOREWORD

Basic Concepts in Psychology was conceived as a series of brief paperback volumes constituting a beginning textbook in psychology. Several unique advantages arise from publishing individual chapters as separate volumes rather than under a single cover. Each book or chapter can be written by an author identified with the subject matter of the area. New chapters can be added, individual chapters can be revised independently, and, possibly, competitive chapters can be provided for controversial areas. Finally, to a degree, an instructor of the beginning course in psychology can choose a particular set of chapters to meet the needs of his students.

Probably the most important impetus for the series came from the fact that a suitable textbook did not exist for the beginning courses in psychology at the University of Michigan—Psychology 100 (Psychology as a Natural Science) and Psychology 101 (Psychology as a Social Science). In addition, no laboratory manual treated both the natural science and social science problems encountered in the first laboratory course, Psychology 110.

For practical rather than ideological reasons, the initial complement of authors comes from the staff of the University of Michigan. Coordination among geographically dispersed authors seems needlessly difficult, and the diversity of points of view in the Department of Psychology at Michigan makes the danger of parochialism quite small.

Each author in the Basic Concepts in Psychology Series has considerable freedom. He has been charged to devote approximately half of his resources to elementary concepts and half to topics of special interest and emphasis. In this way, each volume will reflect the personality and viewpoint of the author while presenting the subject matter usually found in a chapter of an elementary textbook.

CONTENTS

INTRODUCTION

The three terms in the title and subtitle—"psychodynamics," "unconscious mental forces," and "science"—require some explanation at the start.

PSYCHODYNAMICS

Psychodynamics refers to causative factors in mental life. The term, in vogue mainly since World War II, quickly achieved wide usage in psychology and by 1949 had even earned a place in *Webster's Collegiate Dictionary*. Its etymology is both apparent and appropriate. "Psycho-" pertains to the mind; "dynamics" to the action of forces in producing or changing motion—obviously a happy combination for describing the inner workings of the human mentality.

Rooted in the Freudian tradition, the word connotes the interplay of underlying forces which influence behavior in its broadest sense. Perceptions, thoughts, feelings, and actions are all caught up in this vast network of influence, and only when the forces themselves are laid open to scrutiny, can the accompanying behavior be fully understood. Such scrutiny is difficult at best because the processes often take place at an *unconscious* level, where detection is possible only by inference.

UNCONSCIOUS MENTAL FORCES

Nowadays it is trite to assert the existence of unconscious mental life. We are all aware that dreams have hidden meaning and that slips of the tongue are not accidental. We know that hypnotized individuals can later carry out bizarre suggestions without any conscious realization of the basis for their odd behavior. Neurotic symptoms and even many physical ailments are acknowledged to have deeper psychological significance. It is possible to share almost firsthand the excitement of Freud's discoveries by reading Ernest Jones's (1953, 1956, 1957) penetrating biography or simply by watching the pioneer psychoanalyst portrayed à la Hollywood. Nor does it take many hours of TV viewing to appreciate how widespread is the public's exposure to the idea of the unconscious determination of behavior.

As one becomes acquainted with the field of psychodynamics, an important distinction to keep in mind, rather than the obvious conscious-unconscious one, is between unconscious and *preconscious* levels of mental life. Not everything beyond the realm of momentary conscious awareness can be assumed to have the dynamic quality ascribed to the unconscious. Much of what we are unaware lies dormant only because attention does not lead in those directions. Preconscious thoughts are defined as readily accessible to consciousness when attention is shifted to them. By contrast, unconscious ideas resist conscious expression because of their basic unacceptability.

SCIENTIFIC CONSIDERATIONS

The remaining term in the subtitle is "science." The pervasive impact of unconscious forces, combined with the difficulty of their detection, does indeed make for a high order of drama. But drama must be tempered by science if knowledge is to advance. We will make a concerted effort to balance the theoretical exposition of unconscious mental forces and their influence by presenting illustrative psychodynamic research, drawn for the most part from an ongoing program of studies by the writer and his associates.

Besides the necessity for independent scientific verification of dynamic assertions, there is a real need to improve existing theory. In short, psychodynamics can be viewed as an emerging field of psychology whose fertile content is unparalleled in importance but whose theories and techniques are still struggling to attain fruition.

Permission to use passages from their publications was graciously extended by the following: John Wiley & Sons, International Universities Press, Society for Projective Techniques, Random House and Brill Trust, Journal Press, Garden City Publishing Co., Ronald Press Co., Duke University Press, Gerald Duckworth & Co., and McGraw-Hill Book Co.

It seems like an empty wrangle over words to argue whether mental life is to be regarded as co-extensive with consciousness or whether it may be said to stretch beyond this limit, and yet I can assure you that the acceptance of unconscious mental processes represents a decisive step towards a new orientation in the world and in science.[1]

HISTORICAL BACKGROUND

Although one can justifiably repeat the cliché that it all began with Aristotle, the first systematic statement of degrees of consciousness was offered early in the eighteenth century by the German philosopher and mathematician Leibniz (1714). In his view, nature consists of indestructible elements, or monads, which combine to form compound substances. Leibniz held that perception of elements occurs only unconsciously, just as the splash of a single drop of water may be unconsciously perceived but not consciously heard. However, compounds of many such "tiny perceptions" do reach consciousness. The sound of breakers on a beach illustrates this process of *apperception*.

In the first quarter of the nineteenth century, another German, Herbart (1816), introduced a dynamic theory of unconscious mental functions. He conceived of ideas as forces varying in intensity and capable of attracting or repelling one another. The strength of an idea, following its interaction with other ideas, determines the position of that idea with respect to the *threshold of consciousness*. If a strong idea is compatible with the apperceptive mass of ideas already active in consciousness, it can cross the threshold and fuse with the mass. However, an idea depleted in strength through conflict with those more potent, remains below the threshold in the form of an unconscious inhibited tendency.

Others in Germany, following Leibniz and Herbart, further extended the concept of the unconscious. Fechner (1860) became concerned with thresholds while measuring the strength of sensations. According to Fechner, below the threshold of consciousness are *negative sensations* which exist in degrees, and, in his mathematical formulation, are assigned

---

[1] Sigmund Freud, in a lecture delivered at the University of Vienna in 1915. (S. Freud, *A General Introduction to Psychoanalysis*. Garden City Publishing Co., N. Y., 1943, p. 23.)

minus values. Helmholtz (1866) coined the term *unconscious inference* to describe the relation of perceptual phenomena to past experience. We perceive stimuli not solely in terms of their physical properties, but also in terms of their associations acquired in the course of experience. In this same era, Hartmann (1869) based a whole philosophical system upon the premise that the unconscious is the all-embracing ground of existence, permeating both reason and will, which in his view are in a perpetual state of conflict with each other. (See Boring, 1929, for a detailed analysis of the contributions of the theorists mentioned above.)

It remained for Freud, in Austria, to evolve the account of unconscious mental forces which has had—as he predicted—profound impact upon science and society. Setting the stage was the monumental work *The Interpretation of Dreams,* published in 1900. The founder of *psychoanalysis* [2] explored the contents of the unconscious mind with penetrating insight and painstaking care. He uncovered the role of wishes, insistent forces striving for the conscious expression sometimes denied them, in shaping behavior through devious routes. This feat was achieved by the analysis of dreams, described by Freud as the "royal road to the unconscious." Between 1892 and 1895 he developed the free-association technique, by which patients, under psychoanalysis, learn to verbalize whatever thoughts occur to them, no matter how bizarre. Free association has proven to be an invaluable tool for unraveling the mysterious threads of the unconscious in thoughts which occur while awake as well as while dreaming.

FREUDIAN THEORY

PRIMARY VERSUS SECONDARY PROCESSES

In the opinion of many of his followers (see Jones, 1953), Freud's greatest accomplishment was the differentiation of two fundamental modes of thinking: (a) the *primary process* and (b) the *secondary process.* The primary process is the more primitive mode of thinking, characteristic of the unconscious. It manifests itself most clearly in dreams, but presumably exists as an undercurrent in waking life as well. The jumbled thoughts of the insane and of normal people under the influence of certain drugs illustrate its activity: ideas are guided solely by a desire for immediate wish fulfillment—with no concern for logic, morality, time sequence, causal connections, or the demands of external reality. Thinking at this level obeys the *pleasure principle*—the seeking of pleasure and the avoidance of pain. Doubt, uncertainty, and contra-

---

[2] *Psychoanalysis* refers both to Freud's theories and to the specialized technique utilized in treating mental patients. It is a more technical and restricting term than *psychodynamics.* However, data derived from psychoanalysis constitute the core of the field of psychodynamics.

diction have no place in the primary process. Typically, pictures, which are prior to words developmentally, represent unconscious thoughts. The energy of ideas in the unconscious is said to be "free-floating," so mobile that ideas are easily condensed or displaced. The primitive quality of thinking is facilitated by the presumed fact that the energy follows only the path of greater likelihood of discharge. If direct discharge of an idea into consciousness and subsequent conversion into action is blocked, then an individual seeks indirect satisfaction by recourse to memory of previous gratification in similar situations, or by hallucinatory fulfillment of the wish.

The secondary process, which is the characteristic mode of preconscious and conscious thinking, begins to develop later in childhood than the primary process. As speech and the use of symbols are acquired, an individual's thinking tends to become rational, coherent, and organized. Words come to dominate pictures. Psychic energy is "bound," so that ideas can be directed rather than allowed to ramble in uninhibited fashion. Previously, when the process of hallucinatory wish fulfillment was dominant, there had been no control over prospective events. Now, prospective events can be visualized and symbolically manipulated. The capacity to distinguish environmental from internal stimuli permits the operation of the *reality principle*—the regulation and control of behavior according to the demands of the outside world. Anticipation of probable changes in the environment and of consequences of acts leads to the ability to delay gratification by relinquishing immediate satisfaction in favor of a better-adjusted and more adaptive long-range plan of action.

SEXUAL AND AGGRESSIVE FORCES

The human body has many physiological needs, including hunger, thirst, breathing, defecation, and urination. The process by which such needs are satisfied is relatively uncomplicated: bodily changes lead to specific actions for eliminating the need. The necessity for quick satisfaction of these needs allows little variation of behavior among individuals. Consequently, the role of these universal "tissue needs" in the distinctive shaping of personality is minor. In Freudian theory, two forces, sex and aggression, are singled out as especially powerful and pervasive urges that operate in complex fashion. If not gratified in their original form, they are capable of being disguised, displaced to new objects, or banished from consciousness. Thus, they contribute mightily to variation in patterns of human behavior.

All drives [3] can be characterized as possessing (a) *source*, (b) *intensity*, (c) *aim*, and (d) *object*. The source is described by Freud as

---

[3] The terms "drive" and "impulse" are used interchangeably here as translations of Freud's *Trieb*. Early English translations of the psychoanalytic literature employed "instinct" instead, but its misleading connotation of something inherited, rigid, and

"a state of excitation within the body." Sexual forces have an obvious physiological source, but he interpreted them broadly as encompassing more than genital activity. Other bodily pleasures, such as those associated with mouth movements, and ethereal responses like love and tenderness are all subsumed under the sexual category. In the case of aggression, the source usually can be traced to a personal frustration. If the individual's ability to tolerate frustration is exceeded in a given situation, the accumulated tension can produce an aggressive outburst. For example, a repeated strikeout victim in a baseball game may end up by "blowing his top" at the umpire.

The intensity or strength of an impulse refers to the quantity of energy it contains. Since there is no direct way of measuring psychic energy, the amount can only be estimated indirectly from the number and kinds of obstacles the drive can overcome in achieving gratification. The aim of an impulse is its satisfaction—that is, the elimination of the original excitation. Discharge of the pent-up energy dispels tension and restores a homeostatic condition of equilibrium. *Homeostasis* implies a tendency of the organism to maintain itself at a relatively stable level by means of its own regulatory mechanisms.

The object of an impulse, according to Freud, is an instrument by which the aim is attained. Objects may be other persons, oneself, or anything else in the environment. Generally objects grow out of personal experience and can be modified by circumstances. Sexual objects, for example, vary widely, depending upon the situation in which an individual finds himself. If normal heterosexual outlets are blocked, as in prolonged prison confinement, homosexual choices are often substituted. The fact that sexual and aggressive forces are salient at the unconscious level, yet often are prevented from gaining direct conscious expression, creates a stress in the structure of personality, with widespread repercussions. Freud's conceptual scheme for portraying mental conflict will be described next.

ID, EGO, AND SUPEREGO

Some time after the original differentiation of unconscious, preconscious, and conscious systems, the three major divisions of personality—id, ego, and superego—were introduced into psychoanalytic theory (Freud, 1927). Levels of consciousness were assimilated in the newer formulation as attributes or qualities of the divisions of personality, all of which are said to function unconsciously at least in part.

The *id* has been portrayed as the source of psychic energy and as

---

unchangeable has led to a change in custom. "Force," in our usage, is a general term including other kinds of dynamic influence, e.g., defense mechanisms, in addition to drives.

a container of unconscious ideas; in Freud's words the id stands for "untamed passions," and is a "cauldron of seething excitement." It serves as a reservoir for *libido*, the term applied to the energy of sexual impulses. Unconscious sexual and aggressive ideas originate in the id, which is dominated completely by the primary-process mode of thinking and the operation of the pleasure principle. The process by which those ideas are vested with psychic energy is called *cathexis*.

Stimuli may come to the id either from sources external to the organism or from physiological needs. But its unpredictable functioning can only be inferred, never observed directly. Perhaps the closest we ever come to such observation is in the case of a severly disturbed psychotic person, whose bizarre words, gestures, or actions may reveal fragmented, irrational thought processes and wildly fluctuating emotions.

The mental structure primarily responsible for keeping the id submerged beneath the surface of behavior is the *ego*, which mediates inner demands and outer reality. The ego is the executive division of the personality. Its functions include perception, conscious thought, memory, learning, choice, judgment, and action. The ego must also detect and deal with threats in the environment, as well as dangerous unconscious impulses. To block such impulses, the ego draws on its own supply of psychic energy. The opposition of ego energy to id energy is called *countercathexis*. Anna Freud (1946), an eminent psychoanalyst and daughter of Sigmund Freud, offers a vivid description of this struggle:

. . . impulses run the risk of incurring the displeasure of institutions essentially alien to them. They are exposed to criticism and rejection and have to submit to every kind of modification. Peaceful relations between the neighboring powers are at an end. The instinctual impulses continue to pursue their aims with their own peculiar tenacity and energy, and they make hostile incursions into the ego, in the hope of overthrowing it by a surprise attack. The ego on its side becomes suspicious; it proceeds to counterattack and to invade the territory of the id. Its purpose is to put the instincts permanently out of action by means of appropriate defensive measures, designed to secure its own boundaries (pp. 7–8).

Unlike the id, which is totally unconscious, the ego can function at any of the three levels of consciousness. At the unconscious level, the ego deals with sexual and aggressive impulses originating in the id. By contrast, application of the reality principle, through the secondary process of thinking, takes place consciously or preconsciously. The reality principle is of supreme importance in the ego. This executive division of the personality constantly seeks to *test* reality—to distinguish fact from fancy, the rational from the wishful. Having made such a distinction, the ego must decide upon a course of action that maximizes pleasure and minimizes pain.

In addition to serving two masters, the id and the real world, the ego must reckon with a third force: the *superego,* a division of personality specially concerned with moral standards. The punitive aspect of the superego, approximating what is commonly referred to as a "bad conscience," deals with self-criticism, prohibitions, and guilt feelings. The positive, nonpunitive side of the superego, involved in the setting of goals and aspirations, is sometimes designated separately as the *ego ideal.* Initially a child acquires his notions of right and wrong from what he perceives to be the attitudes of his parents. Acts or verbal expressions punished by parents are incorporated as negative values; those rewarded or praised are seen as positive. Gradually the surrounding culture—other adult authority figures like teachers, the peer group, and society in general—comes to exert additional influence in molding the superego. Like the ego, of which it is said to be an outgrowth, the superego is capable of operating at any of the levels of consciousness. The often irrationally harsh conscience operates at the unconscious level, where reality testing is impossible.

When the superego prohibits expression of sexual or aggressive drives, the ego typically joins the superego in opposition to the id. Submission to superego forces enhances a person's self-esteem. Resistance to them usually results in feelings of remorse and unworthiness. It is possible, though rare, for the superego and the id to be allied against the ego. In such a case, the ego struggles against a feeling of pervasive guilt generated by the superego, and the personality may be overwhelmed by severe depressive reactions.

Energy interactions are presumed to occur within a closed system, implying a fixed quantity of psychic energy. For example, the more energy the ego has to expend in restraining unacceptable id impulses, the less remains available for the execution of its other functions. Similarly, the higher the investment of libido in oneself, the lower the probability that one can establish adequate relationships with others because such relationships employ libidinal energy.

The removal of a mental symptom, without treatment of its underlying cause, can result in the sudden substitution of a different symptom; psychic energy is presumed merely to shift from the original to its replacement. For example, a person obsessed by the thought of being dirty may have a neurotic compulsion to wash his hands over and over. If, by direct suggestion under hypnosis, he is simply led to give up his practice without ever understanding its unconscious roots, the libidinal energy probably will attach itself to some other symptom, such as a phobia about walking along dirty streets.

This *economic* interpretation of unconscious forces is extended also to physical symptoms of disturbance. Individuals whose psychic energy is consumed in the struggle between inner forces may show fatigue and exhaustion without any apparent physical basis. Although psychic energy is not equated with physical energy in Freudian theory, depletion of the former conceivably can alter the available supply of the latter (see p. 63).

PSYCHOSEXUAL DEVELOPMENT

Thus far, our outline of Freud's contribution to psychodynamics has concentrated on modes of thinking, sexual and aggressive forces, and the three-way division of personality functions. In addition, he sought to understand and explain the evolution of unconscious mental processes from birth onward—that is, to formulate a theory of psychosexual development. In tracing this development, Freud placed major emphasis on the molding of adult personality in infancy and early childhood.

Infancy. A newborn infant does not possess an ego. The ego becomes differentiated only under the influence of the external environment. The infant has no awareness of the outside world; his experience consists of changes in bodily tensions, which he feels, possibly, as sensations of pleasure and pain. His first tendency is to get rid of these tensions. Once he has done so—by being fed or made warm and comfortable—he falls back asleep. At this stage, relaxation goes together with loss of consciousness. The ego begins to function when the infant first realizes that something has to be done by the outside world in order to have his tensions reduced. He then longs for persons or things to satisfy his wants (this longing is a condition of *stimulus hunger*).

The distinction between self and environment grows out of experiences of indulgence and deprivation. If an infant's needs are always gratified, he continues to think only in terms of self. Some deprivation is required to motivate the distinction. At the other extreme, too much deprivation also hinders ego development, for a certain amount of gratification is necessary. Theoretically, the optimal proportion is a large amount of indulgence combined with a smaller amount of deprivation. Infantile perceptions are assumed to be based on an oversimple view of the world as either a possible provider of satisfaction or a possible threat. Visually, objects are not sharply distinguished, and images are large and inexact. Since changes in body orientation accompany the primitive perception of objects, movement and perception are not separable from each other. Perceptions arising from different sense organs inevitably overlap. More primitive forms of sensation, such as the kinesthetic, prevail.

The first regulator of *self-esteem* is the supply of satisfaction from the outside. When an infant's drives are thwarted by his environment, he loses self-esteem. The longing for removal of disturbing stimuli, when followed by a reduction of tension, not only restores self-esteem but gives rise to a feeling of omnipotence on the part of the infant; wishes seem to be fulfilled magically. Later, as the infant matures, his growing intellectual capacities lead him beyond mere concern with indulgence or deprivation. The pleasure principle is gradually, though never completely, replaced by the reality principle.

The infant becomes aware of probable changes in his environment and can anticipate future occurrences. Knowing that certain reactions from parents can be expected as a consequence of characteristic behavior of his own, he proceeds to regulate his actions accordingly. No longer deluded into feeling omnipotent, he comes to share in the seeming omnipotence of adults in his world. Self-esteem becomes contingent upon tokens of love and affection from the more powerful adults, just as it had previously rested, for example, upon the nourishing supply of milk. He masters tension by inducing adult figures to deliver the desired tokens. This strategy, classed as *passive-receptive mastery*, is characteristic of late infancy.

Freud describes psychosexual development in terms of stages. The first couple of years comprise the *oral* stage, in which sucking is regarded as the initial expression of sexual impulses. An infant discovers that excitation of mouth and lips is gratifying even without food. For example, an infant sucks his thumb to obtain pleasurable stimulation of the mucous membranes of his mouth.

In addition to pleasurable self-stimulation, another aim in the oral stage is to swallow or incorporate. Freud hypothesized that the infant views adults primarily as sources of food and has fantasies of swallowing these food sources, thus making adult figures part of himself. Evidence cited for this magical type of thinking includes various religious rites, such as partaking of holy food in a communion service or the belief that one becomes similar to the object one has eaten. The infant's desire to incorporate food sources is supposedly accompanied by oral fears, such as the fear of being eaten. The prevalence of this theme in literature written for young children, as well as in everyday comments innocently made by parents ("I could just eat you up!"), suggests that these hypothesized fantasies about devouring or being devoured by others are not as farfetched as they may seem at first.

Later in the oral period, when teeth appear, still another aim gains expression. A child who is frustrated, usually in relation to feeding, retaliates by attempting to bite. While longing for pleasurable union with the source of food, the child may yet, in moments of frustration, wish to destroy it. This *oral sadistic* desire to injure or destroy others introduces complications for interpersonal relationships. The mother, for example, now becomes the object of friendly and hostile attitudes. The coexistence of opposite feelings toward an individual is termed *ambivalence*, which presumably is a characteristic of relationships with others from infancy on.

Early Childhood. Following infancy, a number of psychological advances are made, paralleling motoric achievements such as walking, talking, and control of the sphincters. Increasing independence fosters a change from passive-receptive to *active mastery* because positive actions are gradually substituted for simple discharge reactions. The development of judgment helps this process by encouraging postponement of gratification in the face of realistic obstacles and allowing increased tolerance of tension.

The acquisition of speech allows the ego to plan events in the realm of words. The newly acquired capacity to assign words to ideas makes the ego better able to deal with the external world as well as with impulses from the id. At this stage, a magical belief arises that one can master what one can name. Speech comes to be viewed as a charm capable of forcing the outer world to do those things which have been conjured up in words. Among adults, unconscious remnants of this magical power are said to be found in oaths invoking divine assistance, obscenities, and poetry. (See Dollard and Miller, 1950, for a theoretical treatment of the significance of labeling.)

Freud describes thinking at this stage as a further elaboration of judgments, first between edible and nonedible, later between harmless and dangerous. Through the use of small-scale mental tryouts, helpful delays in action are accomplished. In addition to slowing the basic drive to discharge tension, thinking transforms hallucinatory wish fulfillment into the imagination of prospective events and subsequently into abstract symbols of the events. With these developments, the gradual transition from primary to secondary process is under way.

Formation of the superego begins to take place at this time through the internalization of parental prohibitions. Motivated by fear of punishment and fear of the loss of parental affection, a portion of the ego becomes an inner mother, signaling the approach of situations which threaten withdrawal of love. An everyday illustration is the child who, about to perform a forbidden act, glances at his mother and then cries "No, no" while shaking a finger. Such early incorporated prohibitions, though strong in their threat of punishment, are weak in that they may easily be disobeyed when the adult is not looking. They do not possess a unified, organized quality.

The oral concerns of infancy are succeeded by preoccupations with the *anal* region. Pleasure is derived both physically, from stimulation of the mucous membranes involved in the excretory function, and psychologically, from parental rewards and attention during toilet training. Overemphasis by parents leads a child to value elimination highly, and he learns to control his anal activities for use either as weapons against his parents in moments of anger or as tokens of loving compliance. *Expulsive* and *retentive* phases are commonly observed in the anal stage, just as passive-receptive and sadistic ones characterized the oral. Corresponding to the oral fear of being devoured is the anal fear of harm to contents of the body.

Dominant in the next, *phallic,* stage (ages three to five) is the *Oedipus complex.* This is defined as sexual love, in a more literal sense than earlier, for the parent of the opposite sex, accompanied by hatred and rivalry directed toward the parent of the same sex. The first love object of both boys and girls is the mother, because of her primary role in caring for the very young child. As the girl develops, she usually switches affection from mother to father—a complicated process laden with ambivalent attitudes; for the boy, on the other hand, the mother continues to be the preferred parent in a relationship which becomes more sexually tinged than before. The specific form that the Oedipus complex takes in an individual depends upon his direct experiences. Some factors Freud deemed influential are the prolonged absence of one parent from the home, the birth of siblings who usurp the mother's attention, seductive treatment of the child by a parent, family conflict, and so on.

Interest in the genitals becomes magnified during the phallic stage of psychosexual development. Masturbation and exhibitionism occur with greater frequency. Salient fears in a boy's mind concern the possibility of damage to his sexual organs (*castration anxiety*), based upon actual threats by adults or merely upon fantasies of punishment for wrongdoing. Such fears are easily generalized to other parts of the body as well. The discovery that females lack a penis is considered a further source of anxiety in the boy, whereas the awareness of sex differences on the part of the little girl leads her to react with strong feelings of *penis envy* and a desire to be masculine.

As the stage progresses, the boy abandons his sensual desires for his mother and hostile wishes toward his father because of castration anxiety. The girl gives up her Oedipus complex (sometimes referred to as the *Electra* complex) more gradually and less completely than does the boy. She experiences no correspondingly powerful deterrent as the male's fear of castration. Instead, the girl is motivated by concern over losing her mother's love if she continues to compete for her father's affection. The resolution of oedipal conflicts is typically accompanied by *identification* with the same-sex parent; that is, the boy unconsciously copies the father's characteristics, and the girl patterns herself after the mother. In this process, the youngster incorporates or "introjects" the superego values of the parent as an internalized guide for his own behavior. Freud describes the full-blown superego as the "heir" of the Oedipus complex.

Later Childhood and Adolescence. The years from age five or six to puberty are relatively free of major conflict for the child. Sexuality is de-emphasized in favor of new interests and activities, the ego thus growing more relaxed in its perpetual struggle to contain unconscious impulses. The superego, however, has not yet consolidated its position and sometimes functions in an overly harsh and rigid manner, resulting in obsessive, disturbing thoughts. A gradual adjustment occurs, so that when the child is about eight years old the strictness of the superego has largely subsided.

Possessing a more fully developed ego and a growing superego, the child shifts the focus of his attention away from the family toward the outer world. Playmates, school, books, and other real objects provide outlets during this so-called *latency* period.[4] Exclusive dependence on the parents ceases, and freshly acquired knowledge of the environment makes it seem less formidable than heretofore. The average eight year old, reaching out for friendly relations with others, is ready to be influenced by children and adults outside of his immediate family. Belief in the omnipotence of parents fades as they are compared with various adult figures. In general, the emphasis at this time is on recognizing and coping with reality.

According to psychoanalytic theory, the psychological equilibrium of the latency period is abruptly ended by the onset of adolescence. By strengthening the sexual demands of the id, puberty disturbs the balance, and mental conflicts are again rampant. When the id dominates in these conflicts, there is often an increase in fantasy, frequent masturbation, other sexual activity, and aggressive or occasionally antisocial behavior. If the ego clamps down too hard, there may be a rash of neurotic symptoms, inhibition, and anxiety. The superego can renounce its former alliance with the ego, in which case primitive urges from the id are more likely to gain expression; on the other hand, it may over-react to enforce undue compliance, docility, and the renunciation of all impulse gratification. Given these inner conflicts, it is understandable that adolescents typically manifest such contradictory personality traits as altruism and selfishness, gregariousness and solitariness, indulgence and asceticism.

The threatening resurgence of sexually tinged oedipal fantasies leads the young adolescent to isolate himself and to behave like a stranger with members of his family. Sometimes he is attracted to others of his own age, forming very close relationships. Sometimes the attachment is to an older person adopted as a leader, obviously replacing the forsaken parents. As maturation continues, these parental surrogates tend to have less and less in common with the original figures. Love relationships, even though they may be passionate and exclusive, are typically

---

[4] The question of cultural influences upon psychosexual development should be raised here. There has been considerable controversy over such issues as variation in feeding and toilet-training practices among different cultures and the doubtful universality of the Oedipus complex (see Blum, 1953). The evidence concerning sexual latency has been called into question in our own culture by a number of studies indicating sexual interest and activity during this age period. Freud's contention of relative deemphasis in sexuality can probably be described more precisely as an increased emphasis on nonsexual behavior rather than any sharp decrease in underlying sexual concern.

of short duration. Persons selected as love objects are often abandoned without consideration for their feelings; yet the intense nature of the tie is preserved with successive substitutes.

Following this early-adolescent, narcissistic type of relationship, in which selfish interests predominate, there is often a temporary phase of homosexual object choice. Social factors contribute to this development, for adolescents may prefer to meet in same-sex gatherings to avoid the exciting presence of the opposite sex and still not be alone. Friendships initially formed on this basis, in hope of avoiding sexual relationships, may themselves assume a sexual character. Normally, as adolescence progresses, physiological attraction to the opposite sex asserts itself more strongly and heterosexual attachments prevail.

Adult Character Structure. It was Freud's view that the pattern of an individual's experiences, especially during the formative years of infancy and early childhood, determines his *adult character*—defined as the ego's habitual mode of dealing with the external world, the id, and the superego. Success or failure in meeting the numerous crises of psychosexual development leaves its indelible mark. Unresolved conflicts, at any stage, linger on as *fixations* which shape adult personality to a significant degree. Accordingly, psychoanalytic theory delineates a series of character types, reflecting features associated with the various psychosexual stages.

The *oral character* is said to be extremely dependent on others for the maintenance of his self-esteem. He yearns passively for the all-important external supplies. The mouth has an unusually prominent role. Love and food tend to be equated. When depressed, he eats to reassure himself. Other oral preoccupations center around drinking, smoking, and kissing. Marked digestive effects, such as the increased secretion of gastric juices in peptic ulcer cases, are also ascribed to oral fixations. The passive-receptive orientation to life makes gifts assume exaggerated worth as tokens of affection. A demanding tone prevails; there is an insatiable need for reassurance. At times the oral character may overcompensate for his unconscious passive longings by behaving in an extremely active and masculine manner, under the pretense of being completely independent.

The *anal character*, whose traits stem from conflicts over elimination and retention, is described as overly frugal, obstinate, and orderly. Frugality is a continuation of the habit of anal retentiveness, motivated sometimes by the fear of losing a valued possession, sometimes by physiological pleasure. At the unconscious level, feces tend to be equated symbolically with money, so that the extremes of hoarding or wasteful extravagance are commonplace. Obstinacy, a passive form of aggression, corresponds to the child's refusal to produce when his parents were intent upon his doing so. On the other hand, excessive orderliness, punctuality, and neatness presumably arise from compliance and obedience to parental demands in the toilet-training situation.

The *phallic character* reacts against his underlying castration anxiety by behaving in a reckless, seemingly self-assured fashion. Overtly courageous acts—by the motorcycle daredevil, for example—are said to belong in this category. Unresolved childhood preoccupation with the penis is reflected in men by intense vanity, exhibitionism, and sensitiveness. Wounded pride often results either in cold reserve, deep depression, or lively aggression. This basically narcissistic orientation precludes the establishment of mature relationships with others. The male, though driven to attempts to demonstrate his masculinity, is contemptuous and hostile toward women, and incapable of feeling love. The phallic female, also narcissistic, is motivated by penis envy to assume a masculine role and strives for superiority over men.

Finally there is the *genital character*, who has passed successfully through the psychosexual crises without being plagued by remnants of early conflicts. Sexual and psychological maturity makes possible mutually fulfilling relationships with the opposite sex. Emotions are used constructively by the ego as part of the total personality. Love can be fully developed, and ambivalences are easily overcome. Admittedly, the concept of the genital character applies to the ideal rather than the norm.

OTHER PSYCHOANALYTIC VIEWPOINTS

Freud, as the founder and guiding force in the psychoanalytic movement, continues to exert a dominant theoretical influence through the legacy of his writings. Alfred Adler, Carl Jung, and Otto Rank were important early defectors, for a variety of reasons, from the orthodox psychoanalytic position. They were followed by a group of neo-Freudians, who objected to the biological orientation of libido theory and turned instead to cultural and interpersonal explanations of behavior; and, more recently, by the so-called ego psychologists, who are interested primarily in the ego as a force in molding personality. The views of individuals from each of these "schools" will be discussed briefly. It should be noted, however, that Freud's emphasis upon the role of unconscious mental processes has remained essentially unchallenged.

ADLER

Alfred Adler (1917, 1927) stressed the view that universal feelings of inferiority are basic to personality development. A child, because of his size and helplessness, inevitably feels inferior to the adults around him. This reaction is sometimes accentuated by parents who neglect or ridicule him, or lack tenderness. The mother's role is crucial, for by treating the child lightly or by pampering and overprotecting him she impedes the acquisition of social skills. The Oedipus complex is described by Adler as an unnatural result of maternal overindulgence.

The family constellation also can intensify feelings of inferiority: the only child, having been spoiled by his parents, devotes the rest of his life to trying to regain a favored position; the oldest child, a displaced only child, is often so discouraged by his fall from power that he does not recover effective use of his capabilities; the second child may be under the shadow of an older sibling whom he seeks to overtake; and the youngest of several may shrink from competition with the others. In addition, physical defects of any kind can heighten the inferiority reaction.

To relieve the feeling of inferiority, the individual unconsciously seeks compensation in the form of power over others. In this quest, a particular life style is evolved which clearly has its origins in early childhood. The pattern of striving for superiority may be successful if the guiding principles are modifiable in terms of the demands of reality. Very often, though, the attempted compensations relate to impractical goals; neurosis is the end result. Because the male and power are equated in western civilization, women frequently behave like men as part of a *masculine protest*.

Besides the direct struggle for power, people commonly utilize another approach to overcome the feeling of inferiority. Through unconscious flight into illness a person can dominate others by becoming helpless and forcing them to adjust to his demands. Actual or imagined organ inferiorities lead to two kinds of reactions: the case of a blind person who develops an especially acute sense of hearing illustrates the substitution of one organ for another; a stutterer who eventually becomes an orator shows that extra concentration may be devoted to overcome an inadequacy. Even genius is interpreted by Adler as an expression of an urge to compensate for a defect.

JUNG

Another early deviant from the Freudian fold, Carl Jung (1926, 1927), divided the unconscious into two parts: *personal* versus *collective*. The personal unconscious contains forgotten memories, suppressed painful ideas, and thoughts not yet ripe for consciousness. Positive as well as negative memories and ideas are relegated to the unconscious because people neglect certain potentialities in favor of others. The collective unconscious refers to the "racial" inheritance of significant memories (*archetypes*) passed along from one generation to the next. These images are discovered through the symbolic interpretation of dreams. Myths are also carriers of archetypes in various cultures. The "mother image" is an archetype universally viewed in association with the nourishing earth, the warming hearth, the protective cave, and the milk-giving cow. The archetype of the father, on the other hand, signifies strength, power, and authority, linked in the imagination with winds, storms, battles, raging animals. The collective unconscious contains the wisdom of the ages and serves as a guide for human development.

Somewhat less mystical than the concept of the collective unconscious is his contribution to character structure which Jung described in non-sexual terms. According to Jung there are four basic psychological functions: thinking, feeling, sensing, and intuiting. Everyone uses all four in varying degrees, but each person tends to emphasize one particular function. *Thinking* refers to active, logical, directed thought and is used to characterize the type of person who meets every situation in a cool, detached, rational fashion. In the *feeling* type, thinking is assigned an inferior role, and the subjective, value-laden approach is stressed. The *sensation* type, weak in intuition, is quick to perceive everything given directly through the senses; whereas the *intuitive* type, inferior in sensation, is intensely alive to all the possibilities of a situation. In Jung's view, the conscious functions of men are usually thinking and sensation; feeling and intuition are unconscious. In women, feeling and intuition are dominant; thinking and sensation remain unconscious. The repressed feminine side of man is called his *anima;* the masculine side of woman, her *animus.*

Jung further classifies people on the basis of two general attitudes, two ways of looking at the world: extraverted and introverted. Everyone has both tendencies, but, as with the four basic functions, one attitude is salient. The extravert lives according to external necessities, centering his interest and attention on the immediate local environment. For him, the demands of the community are paramount. The introvert, on the other hand, is defensive against the external world and stresses his own sub-jective values instead. This classification is complicated by the fact that the conscious attitude coexists, in a compensatory fashion, with the un-conscious opposite one. Conflict arises when, because of forces in the collective unconscious, the unconscious tendencies are stripped of their compensatory quality. Thus, the extraverted person may end up without interests and no longer knowing what he really wants; whereas the introverted individual may become obsessed by a craving for love from others in his environment.

Another Jungian concept is the *persona,* which refers to the role played by the individual in society as he learns to behave in conformity with what is expected of him. Every profession has a characteristic mask, which the member is likely to wear. A doctor, for example, tends to in-corporate the *collective ideals* of the AMA in his behavior. The persona, shaping as it does the face an individual shows to the world about him, serves as a sort of protection of the inner man, which need not be exposed. In general, the well-rounded individual, according to Jung, has a balance between his conscious and unconscious characteristics.

RANK

The third major defector during the formative years of the psychoanalytic movement was Otto Rank (1929), who emphasized the unconscious fear of separation as a key dynamic force. Birth, according to Rank is a trauma—a painful separation from the mother—which creates a reservoir of anxiety, portions of which are released all through life. People view all separations as threatening; their goal is to regain the feeling of contentment experienced in the womb. They find that the best means of achieving this goal is through the sex act. For the male, intercourse unconsciously symbolizes reunion with the mother.

Life, in Rank's view, is also characterized by a struggle for individuality. A child's individuality may be thwarted by his parents, who drag him into conflicts, seeking to work out their own needs. As an illustration, a father may dote on his son because he sees him as a direct successor and heir, thus threatening the child's individuality. Since the son wishes to be more than just a continuation of the father's ego, he may turn to the mother for refuge. For similar reasons, the daughter often leans toward the father.

Rank's character theory revolves around the concept of *will*, described as a positive, guiding aspect of the self, which creatively utilizes as well as controls impulses. Prohibitions by parents and other adults lead the child to mistrust his own will as evil; as a result, when he reaches adulthood himself, he possesses a will whose contents are in part "good" (approved by parents and society) and in part "bad" (disapproved). Resistance to authority, the bad part, is termed the *counterwill*. On the basis of these notions, Rank describes three character types: (1) the average man; (2) the neurotic; and (3) the creative man. The average or normal person is one who has surrendered his own and accepted the will of the group. Culturally accepted reality becomes his own "truth." He keeps his fantasies, whose contents are viewed as evil, to himself and develops guilt feelings toward others because of his hostile thoughts. In general, the normal individual has fewer conflicts but also has fewer opportunities to be creative. The second type, the neurotic, cannot conform to the will of the group and yet is not free to assert his own will. He has to fight both external and internal pressures and winds up at war with himself and society. The third type, the creative man—e.g., the artist—sets his own ideals and guides his behavior accordingly. Fully accepting himself, he reveals his fantasies to the world in his productions. Guilt may exist toward others as well as toward himself but serves as a stimulus for further creative work.

NEO-FREUDIANS: HORNEY

A later group of dissidents from the orthodox psychoanalytic position shares an emphasis upon cultural factors in shaping personality and rejects Freud's biologically oriented concept of libido as a causal agent. Such writers as Karen Horney, Erich Fromm, and Harry Stack Sullivan stress the sum total of parent-child interactions in the early environment.

Horney (1939, 1945), for example, discounts penis envy as an unconscious force in females. Instead, she attributes envy in women to the desire for masculine qualities prized by the culture rather than to sexual experiences in early childhood. She differentiates three main directions which the child can take in coping with the environment: moving *toward* people, *against* them, or *away* from them. When moving toward people, he accepts his own helplessness and, despite his fears, tries to win the affection of others. When moving against others, he takes for granted the hostility around him and determines to fight. When moving away, he wants neither to belong nor to fight, but to keep apart.

Typifying these basic attitudes are three kinds of persons. The *compliant* type shows a marked need for affection and approval and behaves in a highly dependent, subordinate fashion. At the unconscious level, however, he has deeply repressed tendencies toward power and aggression and actually is uninterested in people. The *aggressive* type has a strong need to control others—life is viewed as a struggle for survival. The softer side of his nature must be firmly rejected, since it threatens his whole manner of living. Lastly, the *detached* type is intent on keeping an emotional distance between himself and others, for closeness creates anxiety. An intense need to feel superior arises in order to justify being isolated. In general, the detachment serves as a defense against contradictory strivings for affection and for aggressive domination.

NEO-FREUDIANS: FROMM

Erich Fromm (1941, 1947) disputes Freud's notion that every individual possesses a fixed amount of libido, maintaining that someone genuinely capable of loving himself is also more capable of loving others. In Freud's view the more that libido is turned upon the self, the less libidinal energy remains available for relationships with external objects. Fromm is also inclined to modify orthodox interpretations of the Oedipus complex and functions of the superego. He believes that conflict between father and son has little to do with sexual rivalry but instead is a product of authoritarian patriarchal society, in which the son is regarded as his father's property in opposition to his own wish for freedom and independence.

Authoritarian conscience is the voice of an internalized external authority, such as the parents, and differs from fear of punishment or hope for reward only in the sense that it has been internalized. *Humanistic conscience*, on the other hand, is the voice of the individual himself, the expression of his self-interest and integrity. When the self goes unfulfilled, guilt feelings arise. For example, if a person cannot approve of himself because he is failing in the task of living productively, he has to substitute approval by others. Unconscious guilt feeling thus leads to fear of disapproval. Everyone possesses both types of conscience, but the relations between the two are said to depend upon the individual's particular experiences. A common form of the relationship is one in which guilt feelings are consciously experienced in terms of the authoritarian conscience, while unconsciously they are rooted in the humanistic. (A person may feel consciously guilty for not pleasing authorities, whereas deep down he is guilty of not fulfilling his expectations for himself.)

In regard to personality development, Fromm states that libidinal factors (e.g., oral and anal traits) are a consequence rather than a cause. The stingy person is not stingy because he hangs on to feces; he hangs on to everything, including feces, because of a home atmosphere which is ungiving and conducive to a feeling of scarcity. Fromm's classification of character types consists of the following: (1) the *receptive* orientation, depending on others for support; (2) the *exploitative*, taking things from others by force or cunning; (3) the *hoarding*, which bases security on saving and keeping what one has; (4) the *marketing*, in which people are regarded as commodities to be bought and sold; and (5) the *productive* orientation, implying the development and full use of one's capacities, such as creativity and love.

NEO-FREUDIANS: SULLIVAN

Harry Stack Sullivan (1953) lays heavy stress upon the role of interpersonal relations. Underlying all other impulses is the *power motive*, which operates from birth onward in attempting to overcome an inner sense of helplessness. His interpretation of anality, for example, emphasizes constipation as a weapon which the child uses to assert power over his parents. Long before he can comprehend what is happening, a form of wordless emotional communication (*empathy*) permits the youngster to respond in sensitive fashion to the actions of adults around him. The later Oedipus complex is explained by Sullivan as a subtle reaction to a feeling of familiarity or strangeness existing between parents and child. Because of the differences in sex, which lead to a sense of strangeness, the parent treats his or her child of the opposite sex with "kid gloves." This freedom from pressure often results in greater affection on the part of the child for the opposite-sex parent.

In the course of growing up, three modes of experience are involved in ego formation: prototaxic, parataxic, and syntaxic. The *prototaxic* mode characterizes the first year of life, when there are no distinctions of time and place. Momentary experiences gradually contribute to vague images of the "Good Mother," who creates a feeling of well-being, in contrast to the "Bad Mother," who frustrates. Next, in the *parataxic* mode of early childhood, the undifferentiated wholeness of experience is broken down into parts, which just seem to happen together without any logical connection. (Dreams are an illustration of parataxic thinking in the adult.) The child implicitly accepts whatever happens to him without reflection. He reacts to others on an unrealistic, distorted basis. Words at this stage are used in a highly autistic fashion, having very personal and private meaning for the child.

By evaluating his own thoughts and feelings against those of others (*consensual validation*), the child gradually catches on to the patterns of relationships in his society, and commonly understood responses become associated with the use of certain words and gestures. Through this mechanism he ultimately learns the *syntaxic* mode of experience which is free of distortion. Attitudes toward the self similarly evolve from the reactions of significant adult figures to him, a process described as *reflected appraisals*.

"EGO" PSYCHOLOGISTS: HARTMANN, KRIS, LOEWENSTEIN

More recently the orthodox psychoanalytic movement has shifted from its earlier dominating interest in "depth" psychology to increased emphasis upon *autonomous* or independent functions of the ego. Pioneering in this approach were Heinz Hartmann, Ernst Kris, and Rudolph Loewenstein, who collectively and individually contributed a number of significant papers to the field of psychoanalytic theory. In listing ego functions, Hartmann (1951) includes reality testing, control of movements and perception, thinking, inhibition and delay of discharge, anticipatory signaling of danger, and a synthetic or organizing function. He portrays a *conflict-free* sphere of the ego, which makes use of *neutralized* energy (originally but no longer libidinal) in carrying out its assigned roles. Even aims, attitudes, and interests which had their origin in situations of conflict may secondarily become part of this realm, operating more or less independently of underlying impulses thereafter.

The above theorists (1946) also describe an *undifferentiated phase* of early development, during which both id and ego are gradually formed, in contrast to Freud's view that the ego grows out of an already existing id. In the first years of life there is maturation of apparatuses which eventually come under control of the ego. These emerging ego structures contribute significantly to the course of development throughout childhood. For example, the infant's distinction between self and object is said to be dependent upon the stage of growth of the perceptual apparatus itself. The ease with which control is learned later in the toilet-training situation is also ascribed partly to degree of maturation; that is, the ability to sit up comfortably, to understand the reasons for regulation, and to communicate signals. In the latency period the gradual increase of super-ego flexibility is attributed in some measure to an advance in intellectual comprehension.

"EGO" PSYCHOLOGISTS: ERIKSON

Another important writer on ego psychology is Erik Erikson (1950), who conceives of *ego identity* as a polarity of what "one feels one is and of what others take one to be." The individual who has achieved ego identity feels that he belongs to his group, and that his past has meaning in terms of his future and vice versa. He "knows where he is going." Both conscious and unconscious factors play a part, but ego identity is described as less of a conscious process than is self-esteem. Ego identity is said to grow out of the various identifications experienced in childhood, not as a summation of them but as a selective integration of roles. This process of integration is presumed to culminate in adolescence. When fully integrated, ego identity engenders a new love of one's parents, and an acceptance of the fact that one's life is one's own responsibility.

With respect to psychosexual development, Erikson elaborates the orthodox position by differentiating "zones" and "modes." In the earliest stage the oral-sensory zone is dominated by the mode of *incorporation*, for the infant not only sucks and swallows appropriate objects but takes in with his eyes what enters his visual field, and opens and closes his fist as if to hold onto things. The central conflict in this phase is between a basic sense of "trust" versus "evil." Next the anal zone becomes important, featuring the *eliminative* and *retentive* modes. These new social modalities emphasize "letting go" and "holding on." Conflicts center around "autonomy" versus "shame" and "doubt." Subsequently, in the phallic-locomotor stage, *intrusive* features emerge, such as aggressiveness, competition, curiosity, and the pleasure of conquest.

At this point a brief outline of the material covered thus far is in order. We began the chapter with a short account of the major concep-tions of unconscious mental activity prior to Freud. Then the contribu-tions of the founder of psychoanalysis were organized into sections dealing with (1) the distinction between primary and secondary proc-esses in thinking; (2) his designation of sex and aggression as main underlying forces; (3) the hypothetical division of personality into id, ego, and superego; (4) his assumptions about the unfolding of uncon-scious determinants in psychological development from infancy to adulthood. Last, the views of those psychoanalysts who have sought to modify the orthodox version through the years were presented in summary fashion.[5]

RESEARCH ILLUSTRATIONS

Most psychiatrists, clinical psychologists, and psychiatric social workers regard the widespread influence of unconscious mental forces in guiding behavior as beyond question. Some clinicians, however, are adamant in their opposition to psychoanalytic propositions. One study (Blum, 1949) labeled these conflicting camps as the "Smug Sympathizers" and the "Caustic Critics," neither of which advances the cause of truth by its vehemence. It made a plea for impartial evaluation of psychodynamic concepts by scientifically conducted tests, independent of the clinical situation. Theories require data to support them, and these theories are no exception.

However, there is disagreement as to what constitutes admissible evidence. Psychoanalysts generally maintain that dynamic principles can be meaningfully studied only within the context of the psychoanalytic interview itself—that is, from the responses of patients undergoing treatment. Using the patient's free associations and reported dreams, the analyst attempts to reconstruct the inner workings of his mind. Such clinical case studies are the traditional method for developing and extending psychoanalytic theory, indeed the technique relied upon most heavily by Freud himself.

But there are obvious problems in this approach. The analyst, despite his efforts to remain objective, cannot be considered a truly impartial observer. His own professional training, which necessarily includes a personal psychoanalysis and intensive supervision of his beginning treatment endeavors, invests him with a deep commitment to theory. The degree of latitude in drawing inferences concerning the underlying significance of a patient's utterances is enough to permit the operation of *interpreter bias*, which can itself take place at the unconscious level. Complicating the picture further is the distinct possibility of *patient bias*. There is an often noted tendency for compliant patients, seeking approval from the therapist, to produce material conforming to theoretical expectation. The patient may acquire the biasing information from prior knowledge of psychoanalytic ideas or by picking up subtle cues from the analyst's behavior during the sessions.

Similarly, the success of treatment cannot be considered as validation of the theory which guides the psychoanalyst's interpretations. The many

---

[5] The psychoanalytic viewpoints summarized in this chapter are expounded in more detail in Blum, G. S., *Psychoanalytic theories of personality*. New York: McGraw-Hill, 1953.

factors that go into therapist-patient interactions are more than likely to obscure whatever role a given theoretical orientation may play. Even if it were possible to isolate that role, there are no universally agreed-upon criteria to evaluate the success or failure of treatment, since the goals are vastly different from one case to the next. Nor do present-day statistics, in all their crudeness and unsystematic collection, indicate convincingly the superiority of one method of therapy over others. Given these complications, it is obvious that the treatment context cannot be considered a satisfactory proving ground for psychodynamic concepts. This is not to deny, of course, the essential part it has played in the formation of important hypotheses.

How, then, can one obtain adequate evidence? The clinician has reason to discredit all animal experiments in the area of psychodynamics, pro or con, on the basis of their obvious artificiality and oversimplification. The white rat seems singularly inappropriate as a subject for the study of complicated unconscious mental processes.

Experiments with humans sometimes can also be quite naive in their formulation. For example, an investigator once tried to test the Oedipus complex by asking individuals to rate attachment to each parent on a five-point scale and, on the basis of the responses, decided that the notion was unfounded. If such conflicts did exist in the subjects, it is most unlikely that they could suddenly free themselves of unconscious distortion and respond in a truly revealing manner. It *is* possible, however, to conduct more sophisticated laboratory research with humans and several illustrations will be presented in this volume.

Another popular approach is cross-cultural. Typically, the relationship between early childhood training and adult personality in various cultures is explored by means of observations and interviews, sometimes supplemented by psychological tests. Though the reports are often intriguing, the methods themselves may pose such problems as unsystematic, non-objective collection of data; investigator bias in interpreting the obtained data; undue readiness to describe general cultural types; and oversimplification in attempting to reduce a mass of complex information. A number of widely cited observational studies of children in western society are open to similar charges of inadequate scientific control over procedures. Proponents argue, with some justification, that those situations which permit the richness of human interaction to come under scrutiny necessarily entail the sacrifice of precise methods.

The psychological test employed most often in cross-cultural research is the familiar *Rorschach technique*, in which respondents describe their percepts in a series of ten inkblots. Projective methods in general, presumably capable of revealing inner dynamics to the skilled interpreter, would seem ideally suited to the task but again there are limitations. The highly inferential nature of interpretation of test responses—combined with the opportunity for evasive subjects to produce barren, stereotyped records—restricts the applicability of such instruments for the systematic testing of psychodynamic hypotheses.

A variety of attempts by the writer and his associates to avoid the pitfalls of gross oversimplification of concepts at one extreme and insufficiently rigorous methodology at the other will be described next.

THE BLACKY PICTURES: A MODIFIED PROJECTIVE TECHNIQUE FOR ASSESSING PSYCHODYNAMICS

Projective personality instruments assume that a person, when shown a fairly ambiguous situation involving an individual or a group, can identify himself with a figure in the situation and ascribes his own unconscious reactions to that figure. Thus the deeper, underlying aspects of personality are tapped in a manner which is not feasible with less subtle methods. In order to avert the hazards mentioned earlier, the writer devised a technique specially tailored to test psychoanalytic hypotheses. *The Blacky Pictures* (1950) consists of a series of cartoon drawings, which depict the adventures of a dog named Blacky. Successively, the hero is nursing from Mama; chewing aggressively on her collar; relieving himself between the parents' doghouses; observing Mama and Papa make love; exploring his own sex organs; watching a knife about to fall on the tail of Tippy, a sibling; admonishing a wooden toy dog fashioned in his own image (see Figure 1); watching the parents pet Tippy; cowering before a scolding superego figure; dreaming of an ideal self; and dreaming of a love object. The subject is asked to make up a vivid, imaginative story for each of the cartoons. After every story there are a number of multiple-choice and short-answer inquiry items relating to the specific psychosexual dimension, and finally the cartoons are sorted according to the subject's likes and dislikes. The use of dogs was intended to facilitate freedom of personal expression in situations where human figures might provoke too much resistance—in other words, might be "too close to home." While minimizing the dangers of resistance, the canine medium, owing to the prevalence of animated cartoons and comic strips, still preserves sufficient reality so that subjects can identify fully with the cartoon figures and project their innermost feelings.

Scores obtained on dimensions (oral, anal, oedipal, etc.) permit comparisons to be made—for example, between male and female respondents. In the original study using this technique with 119 male and 90 female college students, the following account of psychosexuality was formulated:

> . . . In both sexes the early stages of development appear to be interrelated to the extent that disturbances at one level are associated with disturbances at the others. In the case of males, castration anxiety, originating in the phallic period, is also accompanied by earlier oral and

anal conflicts. The male typically resolves the Oedipus situation by iden-
tifying predominantly with a father figure and by introjecting that figure
as his superego. Those who depart from the normal sequence by later
seeking narcissistic love objects are found to have strong, unresolved
Oedipus conflicts accompanied by the lack of a positive father identification. The growing influence of the mother in American families is reflected in the proportion of males (almost one-third) whose superegos do
appear to contain more maternal than paternal features. Generally the
superego in males, according to the test data, represents more a threat
of external punishment than an internalized fear of losing love. The setting
up of a positive ego ideal seems to vary inversely with early oral and anal
fixations, and directly with an anaclitic (motherly) type of object choice.

The psychosexual development of the female, as protrayed by the
Blacky Test findings, is more involved. The early pre-oedipal ambivalence
of the girl toward her mother seems to have a pronounced effect on the
entire developmental process. Strong oral sadistic tendencies persist along
with repressed anal sadism. The oedipal involvement is less complete

Figure 1

Cartoon VII (Identification Process) from The Blacky
Pictures. *(By permission of Psychodynamic Instruments, Ann Arbor, Michigan.)*

than in the case of males, since fear of losing the love of the frustrating
mother continues as a dominant motif. The subsequent identification
process is less clear-cut, and it appears that largely through the mechanism of "identification with the aggressor" the girl is able to pattern
herself after the mother toward whom she still harbors strong under-

currents of hostility. Once the mother has been introjected as the super-ego, the aggressions formerly directed toward her are turned inward and result in strong guilt feelings. The disturbed sequence culminates in the greater incidence of a narcissistic type of object choice in females. Penis envy also seems to play a prominent role in the latter connection. (Blum, 1949, pp. 72–73).

The value of any instrument depends, of course, upon its validity in measuring what it purports to measure. The problem of pinning down a fully satisfactory criterion against which to evaluate test responses is a thorny one. For the projective area it is generally agreed that the best approach is in terms of *construct validity*, relating the test to a wide assortment of variables in the hope of establishing a meaningful frame of reference. The current scoring system (Blum, 1962) for *The Blacky Pictures* has been checked against information on siblings, interests and values, family characteristics, perceived child-rearing practices of parents, physical complaints, field of specialization, grade-point average, social perception, interpersonal mechanisms, and other variables.

EXPLORING THE "ORAL CHARACTER": CONTROLLED OBSERVATIONS, RATINGS, AND EXPERIMENTS

An intensive study of eighteen boys and girls in the third grade utilized a variety of methods in testing ten hypotheses concerning attributes of the so-called "oral character" (Blum and Miller, 1951). The criterion measure of orality was the number of nonpurposive mouth movements recorded at various times over the three-week period of the research. Trained observers followed the children individually during eight two-minute intervals as part of a time-sampling procedure. They tallied such activities as thumb-sucking, licking the lips, tongue rolling, and bubbling. This measure was then correlated with the following series of variables, presumed to reflect the orality syndrome:

Extreme Interest in Food. This hypothesis was checked in two ways. One item on a rating scale filled out by the regular teacher and several student-teachers read: "Which children appear most impatient to eat at lunchtime, as if eating were particularly important to them?" In addition, an actual test situation was arranged:

Our measure of consumption of oral supplies was the amount of ice cream eaten after hunger satiation. The children all ate lunch together. The meal, provided by the school, was dietetically planned and ample for all the children. Upon conclusion of a short rest period which followed lunch, they were offered an unlimited supply of vanilla ice cream contained in one-ounce paper cups packaged especially for the study. The carton of ice cream was placed on a table in the center of the room by a female graduate student who supervised the distribution of cups. Each child was allowed to take one whenever he wished. However, only one cup at a time was permitted, and that in return for an empty one.

No limit was placed on how much a child ate. The carton was kept in the room for the entire forty minutes devoted to arts and crafts, during which period observers recorded the exact number of cups consumed by each child. This procedure was repeated daily over three weeks. From these data averages were computed. The range in any one day's session was quite startling, varying all the way from no cups to thirty-nine for a single child. The absence of any parental complaints concerning illness or lack of appetite was a pleasant surprise in view of the inability of the observers, even at the end of the most frustrating days of the experiment, to eat more than five or six cups without discomfort (pp. 289–90).

Both measures of extreme interest in food correlated significantly with the mouth movement criterion.

Need for Liking and Approval. Here the measures included two teacher ratings ("Which children are most eager to have other children like them?" "Which children make a special effort to get the teachers to like them?") and three time-sampling items (approaches to teacher for approval; approaches to children for approval; and attention to observers). All revealed positive relationships to the criterion, though some relationships were low in magnitude.

Dependency. Teacher ratings provided two pertinent items: "Which children do you think are most able to take care of themselves without the help of adults or other children?" and "Which children tend to ask the teacher for help most often, even when they know how to do the task?" Only responses to the former correlated significantly with mouth movements.

Concern over Giving and Receiving. Again a teacher item ("Which children seem most concerned with giving and receiving things?") showed a moderately positive relationship to the criterion. In addition, staged situations were utilized. It was hypothesized that, if gifts and food are equivalent as oral supplies, receipt of gifts should result in less ice cream consumption. On one occasion the children were each given a box of crayons; another time they received seven colored pencils which they had chosen as a highly desired gift in a rating session the preceding day. The results confirmed the hypothesis, the vast majority eating fewer cups on the gift days.

A related prediction held that oral children would be reluctant to give unless attractive supplies were forthcoming.

After the distribution of ice cream on the second gift day the class was allowed to use the colored pencils in a drawing period. Shortly before the end of this session, a strange adult wearing a large yellow badge marked "Pencil Drive" entered the room and made a very stirring appeal to give as many pencils as possible to the poor children of the neighborhood. Each child then went behind a screen and secretly deposited his pencils in the slot of a colorful box marked "Pencil Drive." All the new pencils had been marked with pin points, so that the contributions of each subject were readily identifiable. Unfortunately, this coding system was of little aid since only three in the entire class gave new pencils. The rest of the collection consisted of a variegated assortment of battered, chewed-up stumps with broken points—all without identification marks (pp. 292–93).

This unexpected state of affairs provided the basis for an additional experiment. Theory leads to the prediction that guilt, typically experienced as a deprivation of oral supplies, should bring about an increase in the consumption of ice cream.

> The day after the pencil drive, the teacher agreed to deliver a stern lecture telling how ashamed she was of their stinginess. She was so effective that, before she finished, one boy blurted out that he had meant to give more new pencils and ran to the box to deposit a few. Next the teacher asked the group to retrieve their donations and observers tallied the number of pencils each pupil took back, which provided the data missing in (the above experiment).
>
> To relieve the guilt, the pencil solicitor returned later to proclaim happily that the school drive had been 100 per cent successful. He then apologized for not having announced previously that old pencils were not wanted (p. 293).

While there were no large increases in the actual amount of ice cream consumed after the "guilt" lecture, certain qualitative observations were noted. The five most oral children in the group sat on the table next to the ice cream carton throughout the whole period, in contrast to their usual wandering around the room. Since they had apparently been eating up to maximum physical capacity, it was virtually impossible for them to eat significantly more cups than before. Another exceptional feature was that none of the ice cream was left over by the group of children this time. The number of pencils previously given did not correlate significantly with mouth movements.

Need to Be Ingratiating. Two teacher ratings ("Which children display their affections most openly to the teachers?" "Which children seem to be always eager to help even when they are inconvenienced?") and a time-sampling item (going out of way to do favors) failed to support the hypothesis that the oral character, by virtue of his never ending search for love and approval, behaves toward others in a very ingratiating manner.

Social Isolation. According to theory the oral character should be infrequently chosen by his peers in view of his passivity, his excessive demands for attention, and his hostility when these demands are not gratified. In a private interview each child was asked to answer several sociometric questions to determine his favorites among his classmates: "Which children in your classroom do you like best?" "Which of the children in your classroom would you most like to invite to a party?"

"Which children in your class are you good friends with?" The resulting correlation strongly supported the deduction that orality and social isolation go hand in hand.

Inability to Divide Loyalties. An oral child might be expected to have greater difficulty than others in choosing between two friends, inasmuch as both represent potential sources of supply. Several days after the sociometric ratings, a measure of divided loyalty was obtained. Each child was interviewed individually and asked to make a number of choices between his two best friends as noted on the sociometric ratings and also between his two best-liked teachers. The interviewer recorded decision time plus comments, actions, and expressive movements. Degree of indecision failed to correlate with the orality criterion.

Suggestibility. Three tests of suggestibility (tasting a hypothetical cherry flavor in candy, smelling perfume from a bottle of water, and feeling nonexistent vibrations in a metal rod) were administered individually to each child. One item of teacher ratings was also relevant ("Which children seem to accept the suggestions of others almost without thinking twice?"). Taste suggestibility was the only measure to correlate significantly with the mouth-movement criterion.

Depressive Tendencies. Self-esteem in the oral child is presumed to depend upon external sources of love or supplies. Therefore, the unavoidable frustration of oral demands is said to be experienced as a feeling of emptiness or depression. Three teacher ratings ("Which children do you think get discouraged or give up most easily when something is difficult for them?" "Which children get the blues most often?" "Which children's feelings seem to be most easily hurt?") failed to support this theoretical prediction.

Boredom Tolerance. Very little tolerance is to be expected for a boring, unrewarded activity, since it signifies a lack of available supplies.

In this experiment the child was taken into a room where he was shown a large sheaf of papers containing lines of X's and O's. The examiner then said: "Your class is being compared with another class in another town to see which class can cross out the most circles." After giving the instructions, the examiner added: "There are several pages (the examiner leafed through all the sheets). Don't write your name on the paper. We don't care how much you yourself can do, but how much the class can do. All right, you may begin."

The examiner then left the room. As soon as the child began, an observer casually entered the room, sat at a distance, and recorded all the actions of the subject. . . . The child was stopped after twenty minutes (pp. 297–98).

The results indicated a moderately high association between orality and low boredom tolerance.

In summary, the results lent strong support to hypotheses dealing with extreme interest in food and social isolation; fair support to need for liking and approval, concern over giving and receiving, and low boredom tolerance; no support to depressive tendencies, need to be ingratiating, and inability to divide loyalties. Remaining equivocal were dependency and suggestibility.

But apart from the fate of specific predictions, the findings demonstrate that dynamic concepts are also susceptible to test by conventional psychological methods such as controlled observations, ratings, and experiments. Additional techniques for investigation will be presented at the end of the next chapter.

. . . The evidence is overwhelming . . . that men and women of today live in an 'age of anxiety.' If one penetrates below the surface of political, economic, business, professional, or domestic crises to discover their psychological causes, or if one seeks to understand modern art or poetry or philosophy or religion, one runs athwart the problem of anxiety at almost every turn. There is reason to believe that the ordinary stresses and strains of life in the changing world of today are such that few if any escape the need to confront anxiety and to deal with it in some manner (R. May, 1950, p. v).

THE NATURE OF ANXIETY

Anxiety is a key concept in psychodynamics. Developmentally, we have already alluded to its role in the oral, anal, and phallic stages of childhood. It is assigned a major function in normal as well as pathological processes at all age levels. But what does the term, which is bandied about so freely in our society, mean?

Anxiety refers to a subjective experience of the individual, a "painful uneasiness of mind" (Webster's, 1960). The feeling is easily recognized in oneself and can be differentiated from other negative emotions such as anger, sadness, or disgust. In addition, there is the presence of physiological disturbance. Responses such as profuse sweating, trembling, and rapid heartbeat are common accompaniments. However, this state of heightened arousal, heavily involving the autonomic nervous system, applies equally to the notion of fear. Many writers consider anxiety and fear to be synonymous. Others point out a distinction in that fear implies a known, realistic danger—in other words, a specific object—whereas anxiety is diffuse and unrealistic. Fear also connotes a predisposition for flight or avoidance—motoric responses designed to avert an external threat. Anxiety, believed to be operating at a deeper level, has no such built-in response patterns. Sometimes the symptoms may be so vague and pervasive that a condition of *free-floating anxiety* is described.

Freud used the term *objective anxiety* to cover fear of a dangerous external object, in contrast to *neurotic anxiety* arising from intrapsychic conflict between the ego and id. Impulses unacceptable to the superego can render the ego helpless as it attempts to mediate between unconscious inner forces and the demands of outer reality. When anxiety is generated by the superego's struggle against immoral thoughts or acts, the person experiences a feeling of *guilt*.

30

ORIGINS OF ANXIETY

The fact that anxiety reactions can be learned is evident. Easily conditioned and attached to new stimuli that have no inherent anxiety-provoking quality, capable of being generalized in accord with principles of learning, the response is clearly susceptible to environmental influence. But some theorists hold that the origins of anxiety go back at least to the birth process and possibly earlier, to the prenatal period of development.

Greenacre (1941) points out that a fetus responds with increased heart rate to a startling stimulus such as a sharp loud noise near the mother. Other reflex reactions to discomfort, such as crying if air has been accidentally admitted to the uterine cavity, have also been noted. Marked fetal activity has been produced experimentally by the sound of a buzzer. Such prenatal patterns of experience, she says, can create a *predisposition to anxiety,* an organic potential which may result in more severe response to psychological dangers later on.

The trauma or shock of birth itself is assigned a central role by Rank (1929), who believes that the process forms a reservoir of anxiety, portions of which are released throughout life. Separation from the mother is the critical event. Freud (1936) modifies this position in describing the birth trauma as the prototype rather than source of human anxiety. Rank's view is said to lay too much stress upon accidental aspects of the act of delivery to the neglect of constitutional factors in the individual's makeup. The role of physiological pain as a necessary antecedent is also rendered less plausible by the observation that persons suffering from congenital analgesia, or insensitivity to pain, do experience anxiety (Kessen and Mandler, 1961).

Psychoanalytic theory emphasizes the overwhelming, intense exposure to outside stimulation which the newborn has no adequate way to handle. Thus, separation from the mother is accompanied by a flood of excitation in contrast to the relative calm of the prenatal environment in the womb. Separation per se acquires a traumatic quality, so that later separations of many kinds produce strong anxiety. Freud (1936) comments that three sources of distress to the infant—being left alone, being in the dark, and finding a stranger in place of the mother—can all be reduced to feeling the loss of the loved person. Anxiety is thus a helpless reaction to the perception of the absence of the longed-for object. The situation which the infant regards as most dangerous is one of not having its needs gratified, when tensions become unbearable. The compelling cry of distress elicited by such deprivation represents his best effort to remedy the situation.

The locus of danger is altered as the child passes through the psychosexual stages. In the oral period there is concern over the disappearance of the nourishing object, breast or bottle. Loss of the body's contents becomes a preoccupation of the anal phase. The next transformation of anxiety, in the phallic years, also is linked to separation. Castration, whether viewed as impending in the case of the boy or as already suffered in the case of the little girl, is interpreted as separation from the genitals. Subsequently the differentiation of the superego as an active force in the personality results in social anxiety, exclusion from the group because of asocial thoughts or acts. Ultimately, Freud asserts, this superego anxiety is extended to death itself, with the expectation of punishment for one's sins in an afterlife.

In addition to anxieties over excessively intense stimulation, nongratification of needs, and loss of the loved object, there is the primitive *talion principle* ("an eye for an eye"): the animistic thinking of the young child may lead him to believe that others want to do to him what he wishes to do to them. If he fantasies devouring others, he may acquire the fear of being eaten. Anxieties over physical harm are presumed to originate in this manner.

THE PROBLEM OF IDENTIFYING ANXIETY

For scientific psychology, the significance of anxiety is complicated somewhat by its elusive quality. In order to make use of the concept in empirical research, it must lend itself to identification and measurement. How can the presence and degree of anxiety be assessed adequately?

Since the phenomenon refers to subjective experience, the most obvious approach is to ask a person to report the feeling and its magnitude. People do vary widely in their ability as self-observers, some being very sensitive and astute, others not. Self-reports are probably reliable indicators unless the subject has some reason to deceive others into thinking he is upset when actually he is not. The general class of experience is readily recognizable, although it may be impossible to differentiate anxiety from labels such as fear, uneasiness, dread, or apprehension.

The uncertainty involved in accepting at face value a report of the absence of anxiety is still greater. Apart from the common defensive tendency to consciously deny one's concerns, there is the added difficulty posed by the concept of *unconscious anxiety*. Clinicians believe that an underlying disturbance may be overlaid with reactions, such as symptoms of illness, which obscure the experience for the individual himself.

Certain stimuli, like impending death, severe pain, or bodily injury have general anxiety-arousing properties. But the reaction, even to such typical causes of concern, need not be universal. Stimuli that elicit anxiety can differ markedly from person to person. Making research still more difficult is the often unknown nature of the object of a person's anxiety.

Indirect experimental approaches to anxiety focus on the relationship of a stimulus to the performance of a task. However, attempts to infer the presence and degree of anxiety solely from decreased ability to perform a task, e.g., involving conceptual or motor skills, are unsatisfactory because other motivational states, boredom for instance, can have similar effects. Also, it is believed that manageable amounts of anxiety can actually be adapted to *improve* performance.

Physical manifestations of anxiety have been studied intensively. They include such things as facial expressions of anguish, gestures of fright, and disturbed speech patterns which are highly inferential as far as the subject's inner experience is concerned. Of course some of the more obvious responses, such as impulsively running away from a scene or "freezing" in a sort of paralysis, are unmistakable signs. Physiological investigation has shown the sympathetic branch of the autonomic nervous system to be active in anxiety reactions. Some stimuli cause increased secretion of a hormone, epinephrine, by the adrenal glands. This leads to increases in electrical skin conductance (of which recordings can be taken from the palm), systolic blood pressure, heart rate, and cardiac output—all of which tend to differentiate fear from anger, according to available data (Martin, 1961). But current knowledge in this area is not yet sufficiently advanced to warrant exclusive use of such diagnostic indicators of anxiety. There is also the troublesome finding that, contrary to expectation, the various measurements do not correlate highly among themselves.

In short, we are left with the conclusion that no single method of assessing anxiety is fully adequate. Instead, as has been pointed out (Krause, 1961), some combination of indicators is always required to carry out research on the topic. A multiple assessment approach to anxiety will be illustrated in an experiment presented at the end of the chapter.

FUNCTIONS OF ANXIETY

The most apparent function of anxiety is maladaptive, namely the disruption of efficient ego operation. Interference with perceptual processes due to anxiety makes the task of the ego more difficult in mediating between inner and outer forces. There is less flexibility in searching for the source of possible danger, discrimination and memory are impaired, and freedom of action is restricted. Very extreme momentary anxiety, or panic, can immobilize the individual completely and eliminate the chance of constructive response. When anxiety is protracted, as in the case of combat soldiers succumbing to stress, anxiety symptoms may include excessive fatigue, stupor, inability to speak, amnesia, and bizarre aimless movements. In its most enduring form, severe anxiety can lead to psychotic breakdown. More detailed accounts of the influence of anxiety upon perception, thought, and action are given in Chapter 3.

Moderate intensities of anxiety, however, frequently serve adaptive purposes, and presumably heighten general arousal to a point where the person is more alert, sensitive, and better prepared to meet crises.

Some research (Martin, 1961) has shown that anxiety improves performance up to a point and only after reaching a certain intensity does it have harmful effects. Another adaptive purpose of anxiety is accomplished by glandular and muscular discharges, which act as a kind of safety valve to prevent excessive build-ups of tension.

Some writers, notably Goldstein (1940) and Sullivan (1953), emphasize the constructive contribution of anxiety to growth of the self. The former maintains that *self-actualization,* the creative use of one's talents, comes about only through encounters with anxiety-provoking experiences. New possibilities for overcoming potential threats are said to enlarge the scope of one's activity and to increase personal freedom. Sullivan stresses the importance of anxiety as a positive in addition to a negative, restricting force. By inducing the child to focus his alertness upon those aspects of his behavior that lead to approval or disapproval from significant adults in the environment, anxiety promotes the evolution of the self.

The major dynamic function of anxiety, which Freud (1936) elaborated in his later theorizing, operates at the unconscious level in the form of a *warning signal* to the ego of impending danger from inner impulses. Development of this function accompanies the gradual acquisition of judgment capacity by the ego (see p. 9). Previously, the flooding of the organism with unmastered tension and excitement was experienced automatically and passively as *primary anxiety.* The ability to judge and anticipate a threat results in the *taming* of anxiety through the creation of manipulatable replicas of potential traumas. Anticipatory anxiety alerts the ego that it must cope with the situation in some way.

MECHANISMS OF DEFENSE

The mechanisms which the alerted ego employs to ward off unacceptable sexual and aggressive urges are referred to as *defenses.* A warning signal of anxiety is perceived unconsciously, and defense mechanisms operate primarily at a deep level. The ego typically responds to threat in either of two ways: *blocking* the inner force from expression in conscious behavior, or *distorting* it to such an extent that the initial impetus is largely blunted or deflected. The major defenses in each of these general categories will be taken up next in some detail, since they represent the most widely accepted segment of psychoanalytic theory.

DENIAL

A very primitive means of defending against anxiety is to deny the real existence of the danger itself. Denial is a contradiction of something known or perceived. In a sense the individual "blinds" himself to the unpleasant aspects of reality as a sort of counterpart to hallucinatory wish fulfillment (see p. 3). Probably the most striking demonstration of the mechanism occurred immediately after the assassination of President Kennedy, when people everywhere reacted with utter disbelief and unwillingness to recognize the tragic fact. In general, anxiety over death is often handled by denial, from the child's inability to accept the loss of a treasured pet to the dying man's failure to grasp the inevitable.

The protective function is clear, yet the defense does contradict the intellect and is only utilized readily on a continuing basis by young children or deteriorated psychotics. The infantile prototype for this behavior is closing the eyes so as not to see a threatening object. Childhood fantasies often contain elements of denial. The fearful little boy may imagine himself to be a brave, venturesome warrior. A pathological example is the severely rejected child who grows convinced that his punitive parents adopted him, and cherishes the fantasy that his "real" parents are loving and kind.

As the boundary between reality and fantasy becomes more sharply delineated for the growing child, he is likely to employ words and acts in the service of denial. Anna Freud (1946) describes the youngster who called out in a lamentable voice whenever he had to take unpleasant medicine "like it, like it"—a fragment of a sentence used by his nurse ▓▓ncourage him to think it tasted good. Such dramatization requires a stage in the outside world, so the child's use of denial is conditioned both externally, by the extent to which those around him fall in with his scheme, and internally, by the degree of incompatibility with the function of reality testing. In normal adults the occasional, momentary uses of the mechanism are apt to occur preconsciously rather than completely unconsciously. Perception of threat has already taken place but denial impedes further development in·consciousness. Yet once attention is directed specifically to the anxiety-provoking stimulus, it can no longer be ignored.

REPRESSION

The major defense which blocks inner forces is repression, which refers to the purposeful forgetting or exclusion from consciousness of wishes, impulses, or ideas associated with objectionable sexual or aggressive demands. Repression is not to be confused with *suppression,* a *conscious* mechanism for withholding responses; i.e., an individual, fully aware of a thought or desire, may for some reason decide not to verbalize or translate it into action at the moment. Two classes of repression are distinguished: keeping out of awareness material that never left the unconscious (*primal repression*); and pushing back what was previously conscious (*after-expulsion*).

The rejection of threatening content by the ego is automatic, that is, accomplished at the unconscious level, but the function requires a constant expenditure of psychic energy (countercathexis) to keep the material from popping up. If the strength of the countercathexis is reduced even momentarily, a dangerous breakthrough can result. Such steady drains on the ego's resources seriously restrict the amount of energy available for constructive activities. The continual striving of repressed ideas for overt expression is betrayed in dream content, unusual behavior, slips of the tongue, and other manifestations of what Freud called the "psychopathology of everyday life." Purposeful forgetting of names or facts previously linked in some way to anxiety is, of course, commonplace. The underlying persistence of the repressed reveals itself in the feeling that one ought to know what has been forgotten, that it is on the tip of the tongue, and so on.

Warded-off ideas strive for discharge indirectly as well as directly. New events or ideas bearing a connection to the original repressed material often serve as outlets or *derivatives*. If the connection is sufficiently remote, the derivative is allowed free expression. But if the derivative happens to trigger a warning signal of anxiety, it too has to be pushed back in the unconscious (*secondary repression*). At times, derivatives are alternately discharged and repressed. An example is daydreaming, the content of which can sometimes be enjoyed in a very emotional way up to the point that repression sets in, causing it to be entirely forg⬛ to e Similarly, nocturnal dreams sometimes force their way into consciousness or remain completely hidden.

Repression is considered an outgrowth of the more primitive denial mechanism. It does not operate extensively until fairly late in childhood, since the defense depends upon a clear differentiation of ego from id. By the time of the resolution of the Oedipus complex, however, ego boundaries are well established, and massive repression of earlier conflicts is said to be characteristic. From observation, it appears that widespread forgetting of pre-oedipal experiences, in the latency period, cannot be attributed solely to normal processes of interference with recall, based on the confusing overlap of current and past events.

ISOLATION

Isolation characteristically refers to a process by which the memories of unpleasant impressions or events are deprived of their emotional connections. The idea is separated from its accompanying emotion by a countercathexis, which, in this case, utilizes psychic energy to keep apart what actually belongs together. Thus, the idea itself can enter consciousness while the emotional significance is repressed, unlike repression proper where the idea is kept hidden. Even exceptionally threatening unconscious forces may be translated into words in this empty fashion. For example, a person may speak of his violently aggressive impulses toward others in a completely bland manner, devoid of feeling. The endless philosophical, abstract discussions in which adolescents engage, on such topics as society, marriage, and religion, often represent intellect-ualized attempts to defend against underlying conflicts concerning sex or morality. In one sense, isolation is an exaggeration of logical thinking, which consists of the continued elimination of emotional associations in the interest of objectivity. But the major difference is that isolation, be-cause it ties up ego energy in the countercathectic struggle, limits the flexibility and productiveness of thought processes.

There are also other forms of isolation besides the separation of idea and emotion. Many children try to solve conflicts by isolating certain spheres of their lives, such as school from home. One usually stands for freedom of impulse expression, the other for social conformity. An ex-treme illustration is the child who splits his personality and maintains that he is two children, good and bad, with different names. By this mechanism the good self is able to deny responsibility for the bad self's deeds.

Another kind involves the splitting of ambivalent feelings (see p. 8) toward an individual. The contradiction is settled by loving one person and hating "the second," countercathexis preventing the two feel-ings from making contact. An example is the good mother and the wicked stepmother in fairy tales.

The isolation of sensual from tender components of sexuality is oc-casionally noted in adults. As a consequence of repression of the Oedipus complex, some individuals cannot attain sexual satisfaction in relation-ships with people toward whom they have tender feelings. Prostitutes furnish these persons with an opportunity to isolate the objectionable sensuality from the rest of their lives, thus relieving the necessity to re-press it.

Finally, there is the separation of two ideas which together would lead to an unpleasant emotional response but singly produce no effect. Such a *compartmentalization* of ideas may be accomplished by separation in time, space, or simply in divided perception. Consequently each of the components can be expressed in consciousness without being perceived as a whole which would otherwise create damaging repercussions. A racial bigot who is devoutly religious must keep his discriminatory at-titudes from making contact with religious scruples of brotherhood and tolerance in order to prevent a severe conflict within himself.

REACTION FORMATION

Reaction formation describes a two-step defensive operation in which an unacceptable idea or wish is first repressed and then its opposite is given expression in consciousness. In other words a conscious, socialized, conforming attitude is diametrically opposed to the underlying force which provided the initial impetus by triggering an anxiety signal. An illustration is the excessive cleanliness of the compulsive person, who is struggling against his inner demands for dirt and disorder. Or the overly affectionate individual whose sugar-coated manner belies a strong undercurrent of hostility.

Unlike other defenses, reaction formation is said to involve a change in the total personality which happens "once and for all." The person molds his behavior as if the internal danger were continually present, so that he can be ready should it occur. Thus, heavy reliance on this mechanism is associated with a certain type of adult character structure (see p. 12). The primary use of reaction formation is generally ascribed to young children in the anal stage of development, who react to their frowned-upon soiling tendencies by "covering up" and succumbing wholly to parental pressures for neatness, cleanliness, and conformity.

DISPLACEMENT

Of the mechanisms already discussed, denial and repression belong exclusively to the blocking category; isolation entails the blocking of emotions though the ideas themselves are permitted into consciousness; reaction formation includes repression as a first step. The defenses presented below are mainly "expressive" in that the underlying force does gain some representation in awareness, albeit in disguised or distorted form.

The term "displacement," in its specific meaning as an ego defense, implies the discharge of an unconscious impulse by shifting from the original object to a substitute. For example, a child who harbors deepseated aggression toward his parents may be incapable of any conscious hostile thoughts or acts against them, but instead vents his feelings by smashing toys. The displaced aspect of behavior is often revealed by an exaggerated response to trivial annoyances, e.g., the frustrated employee who "blows up" at home upon the slightest provocation. A less frequent form of displacement is *turning against the self*, where aggressive impulses toward others are redirected to oneself, producing depression and feelings of worthlessness in the process of self-deprecation.

UNDOING

The mechanism of undoing relies on the magical belief that an objectionable thought or desire can be canceled out by performing a particular action. Rituals are executed in precise detail and fixedly predetermined sequence. Usually something positive is done which is the opposite of something done before, as in the case of the individual who feels compelled to turn on the gas jet so that he can turn it off again. The notion of expiation for one's sins and evil thoughts, achieved by carefully prescribed symbolic, religious rituals, represents a magical undoing. There is a basic similarity to reaction formation in that an opposite idea is conveyed consciously, but undoing goes beyond the realm of attitude into actual deeds. It is also possible for the defense to consist of a drive to repeat the unacceptable act over and over (*repetition compulsion*)—the aim being somehow to shake free the painful unconscious meaning.

INTROJECTION

Defensive introjection is the symbolic incorporation of an external object as part of oneself. Thus the ego, in coping with anxiety, is perceived as having the characteristics of the object. The prototype for this mechanism is presumed to be infantile fantasy about swallowing aspects of the environment (see p. 8). At first, oral incorporative fantasy serves merely to gratify desires for food; later it helps to regain the feeling of omnipotence by creating a closer union with the all-powerful parents; ultimately it becomes an aggressive tool for destroying hated objects by devouring them. The early modes of incorporation are not confined to swallowing—introjection can also be fantasied via the eyes, skin, and the respiratory apparatus.

During the period of superego formation, parental morals, prohibitions, and ideals become the objects of introjection. The child takes over and internalizes parental attributes and values in order to still the anxieties inherent in the oedipal struggle. Identification (see p. 10), a mental state, can therefore be described as the outcome of introjection, a mechanism for warding off threat. Among adults introjection often operates in connection with the process of mourning, the bereaved person unconsciously incorporating qualities of the deceased as a defense against the loss.

PROJECTION

Just as swallowing represents the original model for introjection, spitting out unpleasant things underlies projection. The infant's first judgment is said to be a discrimination of edible from non-edible; acceptance is acknowledged by incorporation, rejection by vomiting or spitting. Projection as an unconscious defense refers to the attribution of one's own unacceptable impulses to others. In exact contrast to introjection, an object in the environment is perceived as having the ego's characteristics. Thus the unconscious force gains conscious expression by appearing to emanate from someone else.

The mechanism functions without difficulty early in life. The primitive method of getting rid of pain, by ascribing unpleasant stimuli to the outside world, readily develops into a tendency to project aggression and blame for misdeeds onto other children. The prominent, long-standing use of projection by man is amply demonstrated in animistic mythologies, where human qualities and feelings are imparted to natural forces, trees, stones, etc. The prevalence of social prejudice and scapegoating very often can be traced to this defense, since racial and cultural stereotypes provide a convenient outlet for the attribution of objectionable sexual and aggressive thoughts to others.

For projection to play a dominant role in adulthood, however, there must be serious impairment of the sense of reality. The classic example is a paranoid individual, whose mental life is riddled with the delusions of persecution. His underlying aggression literally comes back to haunt him. Typically the paranoid suffers from latent, unconscious homosexual desires, which lead to the belief that others are continually making advances toward him. He becomes especially sensitized to subtle deviations in people, so that the targets for projection are not randomly chosen but instead reflect some minimal justification, usually at the unconscious level, for the paranoid's charges. Furthermore, the hallucinated voices which he may hear accusing him of "evil" and "dirty" wishes clearly represent projections of his own superego's condemnation of id impulses.

REGRESSION

Regression is a defense involving the readoption of responses characteristic of an earlier phase of development. Confronted by anxiety, stress, or severe frustration, the individual resorts to a less mature, less realistic mode of behavior. A child, in attempting to withdraw from an anxiety-provoking situation, may revert to habits previously associated with a period during which he felt more secure. Thumbsucking and bedwetting are very common symptoms of regression. A four or five year old may react to the arrival of a baby brother or sister by behaving in an infantile manner, hoping to elicit once again the parental attention and nurture currently denied him.

Adults are no less free of regressive longings. A job promotion, suddenly elevating a person to a position of leadership and authority, can be so threatening to an unconscious need for dependency that a psychological retreat is unavoidable. "Baby talk" is another symptom among adults. Even dreams are classed as a regressive phenomenon, turning back from secondary to primary processes of thinking (see p. 2). The most marked illustration is the catatonic mental patient, who withdraws from life by curling up and remaining mute in a fetal posture.

Regression differs in one important respect from those mechanisms already discussed. The ego, instead of actively instigating the defensive reaction, is itself a passive victim. In a sense, regression "happens to" the ego, and a poorly organized ego is more vulnerable. The pattern of regression is said to be dictated by the sequence of psychosexual stages of development. Response patterns linked to earlier periods typically persist, at a deeper level, along with more advanced ones and predispose the form which a regression can take. Thus oral or anal responses may emerge in place of threatened genital behavior.

The predisposition is termed a *fixation*. Unsuccessful attempts to master a particular stage leave their mark as influential residual forces, which again become salient at a later time of difficulty. Various reasons are proposed for the acquisition of fixation points: excessive gratification or overindulgence, so that the stage is given up with reluctance; excessive deprivation, leading to a continuing demand for gratification; alternating or sudden changes between gratification and deprivation; and the simultaneous satisfaction of an impulse and the need for security— e.g., giving a bottle of milk to a young child whenever he wakes up crying in the middle of the night. In general, regression and fixation are said to be complementary—the stronger a fixation, the more easily will a regression take place under stressful circumstances.

SUBLIMATION

In sublimation the ego changes the aim or object (or both) of the id impulse without blocking its discharge. All other defenses are classed as unsuccessful because they make use of restrictive countercathexes; sublimation is considered successful because the unconscious force does find an outlet, though drained via an artificial route. The original impulse, not met head-on by a countercathectic charge, disappears when its energy is withdrawn (neutralized) in favor of the cathexis of its substitute. Typically the outlet for sublimation is a higher, more socially or ethically acceptable channel of expression. For example, strong underlying aggression can be sublimated as socially approved competition in athletic encounters or in the classroom. Artistic activity, such as modeling clay, often serves as a sublimation of unconscious anal desires. Heterosexual aims may be inhibited and redirected as tender feelings toward a love object.

The distinction between sublimation and reaction formation, at times overtly similar in their behavioral manifestations, is drawn in terms of the above-mentioned absence or presence of countercathexis. Since reaction formation entails counter-pressure, the effectiveness of ego functioning is decreased. With sublimation the ego is free to operate constructively and creatively. Fenichel (1945) cites the example of two children who try to work out, in their manner of writing, anal impulses to smear. The one who sublimates learns to write well and enjoys it very much; the one who uses reaction formation learns to write in a very constrained and meticulous fashion. Likewise, children's pleasure in playing with dirt may be sublimated into painting, sculpture, or cooking, or it may lead to the reaction of extreme cleanliness and tidiness.

OTHER BEHAVIORAL REACTIONS TO ANXIETY

The mechanisms of defense outlined above do not exhaust the ego's techniques for coping unconsciously with anxiety. *Belated mastery* refers to the active repetition of a previously disturbing experience in an effort to "tame" the unpleasant emotion. The repetitive quality of small children's games, as well as their dreams, illustrates this phenomenon. The distinguishing feature of such repetitions is that they eventually lead, little by little, to elimination of the necessity for a negative response. By contrast, certain neurotic patterns consist of endlessly repeated acts which alleviate the anxiety only momentarily, without having an appreciable effect on the long-term perception of the frightening stimulus. Such behavior is performed in compulsive fashion and fails to provide the desired assurance of no real danger.

Other active attempts to defend against anxiety involve the intimidation of others by the use of stimuli frightening to oneself; encouraging others to do what one is afraid of doing oneself; or overtly seeking reassurance and support. Even humor can be utilized as a means of cushioning a traumatic impact. By making light of the ominous and turning attention to its possibly humorous aspect, anxiety may be lessened.

Guilt or superego anxiety has a host of reactions associated with it. Confession, the seeking of atonement, acts of reparation all stem from unconscious forces related to moral standards. Seemingly self-destructive behavior can serve to gratify a need for punishment and expiation of one's sins. An individual may, without conscious awareness, place himself in a situation where an accident is likely to befall him. Some criminal acts are carried out in such an obvious manner that apprehension by the police and subsequent punishment are virtually inevitable. These occurrences point to the hidden motivation of a guilty conscience. If the sought-for experiences of pain are sexually tinged or actually pleasurable, the underlying condition is known as *masochism*.

In this chapter we have examined the nature and role of anxiety as a mental force, along with the variety of unconscious defenses against its expression. Following two research illustrations in this area, the next chapter will seek to establish a bridge between psychodynamic concepts and traditional topics of concern in the field of psychology—perception, thought, and action.

RESEARCH ILLUSTRATIONS

AN EXPERIMENT ON UNCONSCIOUS ANXIETY

The concept of unconscious anxiety is somewhat controversial even within psychoanalytic theory itself. According to Freud, the content of the unconscious consists only of ideas. It is technically incorrect to speak of unconscious emotions, since an emotion is something that has already entered consciousness. Only the idea which gives rise to an emotion can be repressed and kept inaccessible. When terms like unconscious anxiety or guilt are used, it is merely a looseness of phraseology. Others maintain that it is legitimate to speak of unconscious emotions in the sense that there may be tensions in the organism which, if not blocked, would result in specific emotions. Fenichel (1945), for example, describes unconscious predispositions, in which an individual unknowingly may have a readiness toward rage, sexual excitement, anxiety, or guilt.

These divergent opinions led to the design of an experiment (Blum, 1961) testing whether *unconscious activation* of an idea highly loaded with anxiety can result in an observable emotional discharge. Several methodological problems were involved in the execution of the experiment: (1) making certain that an idea was initially linked to anxiety; (2) establishing the fact that activation of the idea did take place unconsciously without reaching preconscious or conscious levels; and (3) obtaining valid estimates of the presence or absence of a consequent anxiety response.

The last problem was handled by the multiple approach recommended on page 33. In preliminary training sessions, the measurement of anxiety by the galvanic skin response (GSR), recorded from the palm, was confirmed both by the subject's report of his conscious emotional experience and experimenters' observations of expressive movements. In other words, the subjects, experimenters, and GSR recordings all tended to agree that anxiety was or was not present on any given trial. During the experiment itself, then, the GSR readings were used as the criterion measure.

The remaining two problems were handled by hypnotic techniques, which offer unusual opportunities for precise control over experimental variables: (1) anxiety was linked to a particular stimulus by a *hypnotic suggestion* to feel anxious whenever the stimulus was present; (2) the major hurdle of separating unconscious from preconscious activation of an idea was overcome by training subjects "not to see" a given stimulus when it was flashed very quickly in the tachistoscope, even though they did not know in advance at what point in a series of stimuli it would appear. That is, hypnotically suggested blindness to a particular stimulus only took effect immediately upon its presentation; the perception of other stimuli was not affected at all. In order for the suggestion to be carried out correctly, the critical stimulus first had to be perceived at an unconscious level and discriminated from other stimuli to which blindness did not apply. Subjects were required to guess right afterward which stimulus might have been flashed in those instances when nothing was "seen." Incorrect guesses were interpreted to indicate that perception of the stimulus had not developed sufficiently to reach preconsciousness, i.e., the stimulus could not be retrieved consciously when the subject was encouraged to do so (see p. v). Thus *preconscious* perceptual registration was ruled out. Genuineness of the blindness phenomenon itself was supported by a combination of behavioral and physiological evidence (see Blum, 1961, pp. 59–60).

The experiment consisted of several series of trials in which four stimuli (three dots in a vertical line, three dots in a horizontal line, a triangle, and a blank card) were flashed repeatedly, one at a time, in random order. In Series A the stimuli were shown at a fairly fast speed where recognition was still 100 per cent correct. The same speed was then used throughout the next three series. Prior to Series B, the subject was told hypnotically to be blind to both the vertical and horizontal dots but to see the triangle and blank clearly. The crucial series was C, before which the additional instruction was given: "Whenever the vertical (but not the horizontal) dots are flashed, *whether you see them or not*, you will immediately feel extremely nervous and upset." Finally, for Series D, the blindness instruction was removed from the dot stimulus to which it had been attached (in some cases the horizontal rather than the vertical dots were used as the critical stimulus), but the anxiety suggestion remained in force.

The three male college students who took part in the experiment gave strong galvanic skin responses to the consciously perceived crucial stimulus during Series D, showing that the stimulus was indeed anxiety-linked. In Series C, by means of the method previously indicated, the experimenters separated preconscious responses from unconscious responses. That is, when a subject was "blind" to a stimulus but was able to guess what it had been, the perception was classed as preconscious; when the stimulus was blanked out by the subject and also not guessed, the perception was classed as unconscious. In not a single instance did such an unconscious perception produce a GSR. Interestingly, the preconscious perceptions in Series C revealed galvanic skin responses as large as the reactions occurring in Series D. Series B showed that the blindness instruction alone did not affect the GSR; Series A simply provided a baseline condition in which there was no experimental manipulation.

In summary, results of the experiment suggest that activation of an unconscious idea does *not* release its associated anxiety response, but that preconscious activation can produce as potent a discharge as fully conscious awareness does. Again, apart from the specific findings, the study demonstrates that, given appropriate methods and techniques, the most elusive psychodynamic concepts can also be put to rigorous laboratory test.

COMPARISONS OF DEFENSE PREFERENCES AMONG COLLEGE STUDENTS

In order to assess defensive reactions to psychosexual stimuli in an indirect but objectively scorable fashion, an adaptation of the Blacky Pictures technique (see p. 23) was constructed. This *Defense Preference Inquiry* (DPI) consists of a series of five alternative statements following the presentation of each of eleven pictures. The subject is asked simply to rank the items in each set from 1 to 5 in terms of "how well they

Table I

International comparisons of defense preferences among male college students. (From Blum, 1964, p. 15.)

LEGEND: PREFERENCE (+)   NEUTRAL (○)   AVERSION (—)

Blacky Dimension		Avoidance				Reaction Formation				Projection				Regression				Intellectualization			
		Is	Fr	Dk	Ger	Is	Fr	Dk	Ger	Is	Fr	Dk	Ger	Is	Fr	Dk	Ger	Is	Fr	Dk	Ger
(Oral Eroticism)	I	—	+	+	—	—	—	○	○	+	+	—	○	+	+	○	+	+	+	—	○
(Oral Sadism)	II	○	○	+	○	○	—	○	—	—	—	—	○	+	+	+	+	+	+	○	○
(Anal Sadism)	III	○	+	+	○	—	—	○	—	—	○	—	○	○	—	—	○	+	+	+	+
(Oedipal Intensity)	IV	+	+	+	+	+	+	+	○	+	+	+	+	—	○	—	○	—	—	—	—
(Masturbation Guilt)	V	+	○	+	+	○	○	+	+	+	+	○	○	—	—	—	—	+	+	○	○
(Castration Anxiety)	VI	○	+	○	○	○	+	+	+	○	+	○	○	—	○	○	○	○	—	○	—
(Overt Aggression)	VII	—	—	+	○	+	+	+	○	○	○	+	+	○	+	—	○	—	○	—	○
(Sibling Rivalry)	VIII	+	○	○	—	○	○	○	○	—	—	○	+	—	—	—	+	○	+	○	○
(Guilt Feelings)	IX	○	○	+	○	○	○	○	○	—	○	○	—	+	—	—	—	—	+	+	○
(Ego Ideal)	X	○	○	+	+	+	+	○	○	—	—	○	○	—	—	—	—	+	+	○	+
(Love Object)	XI	+	+	+	+	—	○	○	+	—	—	—	—	○	+	○	○	○	+	○	—

represent the way Blacky seems to be feeling or acting" in that picture. The subject is thus encouraged to identify with Blacky and thereby reveal his own personal reactions. Spontaneity of response is facilitated by very short time limits, which preclude the possibility of careful deliberation in assigning the ranks.

The same five defenses appear in each of the eleven sets of alternatives: reaction formation, projection, regression, intellectualization, and avoidance (a general term referring to the repression-denial family). Here are two illustrative items from the Oral Sadism picture, which shows Blacky chewing vigorously on Mama's collar:

"When Blacky gets angry, he often throws a temper tantrum like he did in his earlier days." (Regression)

"Blacky is so intent on chewing the collar to pieces that he doesn't even realize it belongs to Mama." (Avoidance)

Attempts to check the meaningfulness of DPI responses among college students have concentrated on a construct validity type of approach (see p. 25). For example, avoidance choices in the case of some Blacky pictures have been shown to relate to greater forgetting of the relevant pictures themselves in a series of picture-recall tests. In word-completion and anagram tasks, avoidance was accompanied by the selection of neutral rather than conflict-associated solutions (e.g., selecting a "v" rather than a "c" to complete in est). Two individuals who shared the first choice of projection in a given psychosexual area tended to have predictably more negative interpersonal dealings than was usual, when paired with one another in a cooperative task (Cohen, 1956). In this experiment, both members of a pair were given a story whose content lay in the relevant psychosexual area. Each subject was asked to write his own interpretation of the motivation of the main character in the story. Next, they were asked to discuss the story for fifteen minutes, preparatory to writing a joint interpretation. Afterward, each was required, privately, to judge how well he and his partner had interacted. Ratings by paired projectors turned out to be more negative than those made by people utilizing other defenses.

Another line of investigation employing the DPI has involved the comparison of responses of male samples at universities located in eight countries (Blum, 1956, 1964). An initial study in 1955 included England, Italy, the Netherlands, and the United States; a follow-up in 1962 added Denmark, France, West Germany, and Israel. Both phases revealed the variability of preferences *among the individuals* of a given country to be as great as the variability *between countries*. In other words, within-country heterogeneity casts serious doubt upon the popular pastime of indulging in national stereotypes. The few national trends which did emerge consistently were a strong preference for avoidance in the Dutch and Danish samples, and for intellectualization in the French group. The accompanying table presents, in summary form, the preferences, on each Blacky dimension, obtained in the follow-up study employing the Defense Preference Inquiry.

. . . Again the atoms were gamboling before my eyes. This time the smaller groups kept modestly in the background. My mental eye, rendered more acute by repeated visions of this kind, could now distinguish larger structures, of manifold conformation; long rows, sometimes more closely fitted together; all twining and twisting in snakelike motion. But look! What was that? One of the snakes had seized hold of its own tail, and the form whirled mockingly before my eyes. As if by a flash of lightning I awoke . . .[1]

Three broad processes of traditional concern to psychology are perceiving, thinking, and acting. Unconscious mental forces play a vital role in shaping these processes. Our purpose now is to make this role clear by presenting illustrations of the effects of sexual and aggressive impulses, anxiety, and defensive reactions on the three processes. Each discussion begins with pathological effects, since abnormal manifestations tend to be especially vivid.

INFLUENCES UPON PERCEPTION

PATHOLOGICAL EFFECTS

Unconscious interference with the execution of perceptual functions runs the gamut of: complete momentary disruption, as in fainting; serious long-term partial impairment—e.g., hysterical blindness; recurrent psychotic hallucinations; and minor symptoms of distractibility.

Fainting is regarded as the total collapse of the ego in response to a trauma. A major ego function, consciousness, is given up, resulting in inability to perceive the traumatic threat or to act. By this inability to perceive, the individual is prevented from being exposed further to the threatening stimuli. Such temporary relief from overwhelming stimulation is described as the most primitive defense mechanism, for consciousness itself is sacrificed by the ego in order to ward off additional anxiety. A familiar example is an individual who, because of severe underlying anxiety over personal injury, passes out upon the sight of his own blood. Physiologically, traumatic experiences produce fainting through their effect upon the vasomotor system. General vasodilatation

---

[1] Thus Fredrich Kekule described a dream episode that led to the solution of a significant problem: the chemical structure of the benzene molecule—a closed ring of six carbon atoms to each of which a hydrogen atom is attached. (Findlay, A. *A Hundred Years of Chemistry*, 3rd ed.), London: Duckworth, 1948, p. 39.)

and a profound drop in blood pressure occur, causing temporary anemia of the brain.

Hysterical blindness is a functional disorder, which means that there is no physical, organic basis for it.[2] The eyes themselves are normal— as evidenced by the fact that the hysterically blind person is able to dodge obstacles in his path. The organically blind walks carefully but stumbles over obstructions; and the simulator, who for some reason deliberately pretends to be blind, will usually knock himself into things intentionally to prove his case. Dynamically, the explanation of functional blindness often lies in the unconscious sexualization of looking, as in *voyeurism*. Hidden erotic desires to view forbidden objects become so threatening that loss of vision is unconsciously resorted to as a counter measure. This mechanism is classed as a *conversion reaction*, in which a specific body function expresses an unconscious conflict in symbolic form. Freud invokes the talion principle (see p. 32) in pointing out that the sinning organ, the eye, is punished by being rendered useless. The fable of the peeper who was struck blind after spying on Lady Godiva fits this description. Blinding oneself in an effort to relieve guilt was given literary expression as long ago as the ancient Greek era. Oedipus Rex, in Sophocles' play, destroyed his own sight upon discovering that he had committed incest unknowingly. Aggressive as well as sexual impulses linked to the eye can also underlie the hysterical malfunction. A person overwhelmed by hostile impulses whenever he sees someone he hates can conceivably defend against the dangerous discharge of those impulses by losing his sight. Expressions like "blind with rage," "the evil eye," and "if looks could kill" attest to the emotional significance attached to vision.

Hallucinations are sense experiences in the absence of external stimuli: inner ideas are projected and experienced as if they were actual perceptions. Such breakdowns in the function of reality testing (see p. 3) often take place in schizophrenic patients, but they can also be induced artificially by drugs, hypnosis, or sensory isolation. The content of naturally occurring hallucinations in the psychotic individual typically represents either a wish fulfillment or the projection of painful ideas. We have already cited the illustration (p. 40) of paranoid schizophrenics, who characteristically hear voices accusing them of perverse sexual desires. The most common mode for psychotic hallucinations is auditory, with visual somewhat less frequent. Taste, smell, and tactile hallucinations also appear occasionally.

A minor everyday manifestation of the influence of psychodynamic forces upon perception can be noted in some forms of distractibility. If

---

[2] The hypnotic induction of blindness (see p. 43) also falls into the functional category, of course.

a task on which concentration is required somehow stirs up anxiety, an individual's attention may be unconsciously diverted. For example, when an instructor is lecturing on an emotionally loaded topic, a student may suddenly find himself gazing vacantly out the window instead of taking down the notes. Also, some neurotic persons experience a pathological need for outer distractions, such as a constantly loud-playing radio, in order to take their minds off inner anxieties.

THE INFLUENCE OF NEEDS AND VALUES

A number of experiments have demonstrated the influence of underlying needs and values upon perceptual processes, particularly when the perceived stimuli are ambiguous (see Weintraub and Walker, 1966, for a systematic review). For example, hunger, manipulated by deprivation of food for varying numbers of hours, has resulted in the "perception" of more food-related items in ambiguous drawings or on a blank screen where subjects were led to believe that faint visual cues were present; a tendency to supply missing letters in words in favor of food rather than non-food alternatives; and lowered recognition thresholds for food-related words. A series of experiments employing both hunger and thirst revealed that deprived subjects, when asked to judge the brightness of previously projected images of food or drink objects, consistently made brighter illuminance matches than did nondeprived control subjects. Similar experiments have been carried out with the arousal of sexual motives, noting their effect upon responses to ambiguous pictorial stimuli (Clark, 1952).

The influence of personal values has also been a favorite topic for investigation. The bulk of the evidence suggests that preferred personal values (usually classified according to the categories of theoretical, economic, political, esthetic, religious, and social) lead to lowered recognition thresholds for moderately unfamiliar, relevant words. In short, both needs and values can operate unconsciously to make a person attribute subjective meaning to stimulus conditions.

EFFECTS UPON JUDGMENTS OF SIZE AND SPACE

Highly valued objects tend to be judged larger in size than they really are (Jenkin, 1957). This finding derives from a variety of studies employing such stimuli as coin size (overestimation increases with value of coins); poker chips associated with a candy reward; and pictures of personally preferred food objects. Though any single study may be open to methodological criticism, the general tenor of the results in this area is impressive. Even weights have been used to demonstrate the phenomenon of overestimation: children estimate the weight of valued objects (jars filled with candy) as heavier than neutral objects (jars filled with sand and sawdust). Investigations (Holzman and Klein, 1956) more directly relevant to the field of psychodynamics have linked certain defense mechanisms to the judgment of size. Subjects who relied most upon isolation for defensive purposes were more accurate in their estimates and also preserved subtle differences in apparent sizes of discs ("focusers"); those who relied most upon repression were inaccurate and tended to blur distinctions ("non-focusers").

Spatial judgments have also been shown to be susceptible to underlying forces. Psychosexually disturbing stimuli, assessed from individual responses to the Blacky pictures, were typically seen as more remote or smaller than neutral stimuli, regardless of accompanying defense preferences (Shellow, 1956). In the rod-and-frame test, a subject is placed in a darkened room and is required to observe a luminous rod within a tilted frame, and to judge when the rod is vertical (Witkin et al., 1954). Generally, anxious persons give characteristic responses to the test. Such individuals tend to base their estimates very largely on visual surroundings (*field-dependent*) rather than on the cues from their own bodies (e.g., gravitational ones), which are less likely to lead to distortion (*field-independent*).

The perceptual phenomenon of *size constancy*—by which objects appear the same size regardless of their distance (for example, a chair 10 feet away does not look perceptibly smaller than an identical chair 2 feet away, although the retinal image of the latter is five times as large as the former)—also seems to vary with personality attributes (Raush, 1952). Paranoid schizophrenics yielded higher constancy scores than a normal control group. This "over-constancy" was interpreted as an unconscious means of compensating for threats to the stability of the individual's ego structure, by the projection of an artificial stability onto the environment.

EFFECTS OF UNCONSCIOUS RESISTANCE AND SELECTIVITY: PERCEPTUAL DEFENSE AND VIGILANCE

The phenomenon of *perceptual defense* refers to an unconscious resistance to recognition of threatening stimuli. Such motivated difficulty in perceiving is analogous to repression in the realm of memory (see MacKinnon and Dukes, 1962, for a review and evaluation of research in both areas). The concept has generated a large number of experiments and an accompanying storm of controversy following its introduction in the late 1940s. Initially, the studies typically involved tachistoscopic presentation of neutral and socially taboo words. For the latter, galvanic skin responses (GSRs) and higher recognition thresholds were observed. The "defense" interpretation (that is, that the subjects were manifesting unconscious reactions due to anxiety) was promptly challenged on a number of counts: (1) taboo words are lower in frequency of usage, therefore less familiar and not so easily identified; (2) the stimuli actually may be perceived, but subjects, because of the social settings of the experiments, are unwilling to verbalize them; (3) stronger, competing tendencies are more likely responsible for the effect; (4) the GSR cannot be considered an indicator of subliminal registration of stimuli, since it may be produced instead by conflict of response tendencies; (5) the explanation smacks of a "little man inside the head" who decides in advance what should or should not be seen.

In a series of experiments in our laboratory at the University of Michigan, we sought to relate the phenomenon and its associate, *perceptual vigilance,* more closely to dynamic principles of unconscious mental functioning. Vigilance, or selective sensitization, was linked to the tendency for sexual and aggressive impulses actively to seek an outlet and break through into consciousness. This process can be expected to operate only at a level below awareness; for, once the unacceptable impulses begin to approach the surface, a second process—*ego defense*—attempts to avert their threatening expression by means of countercathexis.

Accordingly, an experiment was devised to demonstrate the conditions for occurrence of vigilance and defense (Blum, 1954). The following conditions were set up: (1) a pretest, baseline series of trials involving simultaneous tachistoscopic presentations of four Blacky pictures at a very fast speed (.03-second duration)—the subject being asked only to indicate the position (left, right, top, or bottom) of the picture which "stood out the most"; (2) a sensitization procedure, during which two of the stimulus pictures were presented in full view and their contents explained so that one was structured as *threatening* (designed to elicit psychosexually disturbing thoughts) and the other as *neutral;* (3) a test series identical to the previous baseline condition; and (4) a test presentation at a slower speed (.20-second duration) approaching the level of conscious recognition—the subject being instructed to locate the position in which a particular picture appeared (designed to introduce ego defensiveness both by having the more slowly exposed stimuli closer to consciousness and also by requiring the subject to label them directly). As predicted, fewer correct locations were selected for the emotionally loaded than the neutral pictures in the defense series (Condition 4); whereas the position of the loaded picture was selected as standing out more often than the other three positions in the briefly exposed vigilance series (Condition 3), supporting the view that impulses actively seek outlet. Subsequent attempts by others to replicate these findings have resulted in confirmation of the vigilance, but not the defense, effect (Smock, 1956); evidence for both in an extension using prior psychological assessment of individual conflicts and defense preferences (Nelson, 1955); and a demonstration of the significance of stimulus duration in an experimental design employing the same task at both speeds—selecting the "clearest" of the four pictures (Mattson and Natsoulas, 1962).

A willingness to grant the existence of perceptual defense (which had long before gained clinical acceptance in the phenomenon of hysterical blindness discussed on page 49) still leaves unanswered the intriguing question concerning the mechanism by which it is carried out. Obviously the "little man inside the head" notion is absurd. But if we conceive of the subject's response as the culmination of a perceptual-cognitive sequence—beginning with sensory registration of the stimulus, followed by central processing, which leads to the verbal report—the possibility of interference and disruption along the way no longer seems quite so far-fetched. The assumption that discrimination can occur without awareness is rendered especially plausible by the efficacy of the selective, hypnotically induced blindness described on page 43. Stimuli can register and yet not develop fully enough along the perceptual-cognitive sequence to enter consciousness in the form of percepts. Somewhat more uncertain is whether the interference is due simply to a stronger, competing "hypothesis," which takes over as a distraction and usurps conscious attention (Postman, 1953), or whether there is a direct, active inhibitory process triggered by the anxiety-laden stimulus.

Several of our studies have supported the direct-inhibition interpretation. One experiment involved the perceptual task of naming four Blacky pictures, which were flashed simultaneously at a tachistoscopic speed well below conscious awareness (Blum, 1955). Subjects previously assessed as showing conflict over a particular picture, combined with and having a preference for repression in the relevant psychosexual area, tended to make fewer calls of that picture than of accompanying neutral ones. Since the experimental design made it possible to control the three variables: (1) suppression of verbal report, (2) familiarity with the stimuli, and (3) predisposition to respond in set ways, the resulting avoidance tendency could be linked directly to the perceptual process itself. Subsequent investigations (Blum, 1957, 1961; Perloe, 1960) have reinforced the notion of an active inhibitory mechanism.

INFLUENCES UPON THOUGHT

PATHOLOGICAL EFFECTS

Just as unconscious mental forces distort the process of perceiving, the range of their influence can also be observed in the realm of thought. A prominent neurotic symptom is the *obsession,* a persistent, recurring thought which the afflicted individual is unable to shake. Sometimes such ideas reflect thinly disguised underlying impulses; for instance, the wife who is perpetually afraid that some harm will come to her husband actually may harbor strong unconscious hostility toward him. More often, obsessions represent commands of the superego and are defensive or self-punishing. Obsessive doubting and rumination, typically centering on abstract intellectual speculation over problems like right and wrong or the meaning of life, can usually be traced to an unconscious conflict about a forbidden idea. Whatever the obsessional form, the energy behind the recurring symptom is said to derive from the underlying impulse whose threatening expression has been warded off. Similar mechanisms can be at work in the normal individual, but there is a distinct quantitative difference compared to the endless preoccupation of the neurotic with a particular thought.

Another common disorder in the thinking process is the *delusion,* a fixed belief that persists in contradiction to reality. It is analogous to hallucination, in that the misjudgment of external reality is based largely on projection, sometimes of a wish-fulfilling nature but more often painful and frightening. Delusions of persecution by other individuals are very frequent among psychotics, especially those suffering either from paranoia or paranoid schizophrenia. Freud traced the basic conflict in such cases to latent homosexuality—the first defensive step being unconscious denial of the sexual impulse ("I do not love him, I hate him"), followed by projection ("He hates me"). Delusions of grandeur are noted less often, as when a paranoid person comes to view himself as a religious prophet or scientific genius in order to defend against total ego disintegration. Though delusions vary in their content and degree of systematization, the individual is always convinced that his belief is based upon actual fact.

Disorganization of thought processes is characteristic of some schizophrenic reactions. In the face of overwhelming emotional stress, prelogical thinking regressively dominates mental activity, as it did in early childhood. Conventional sequences of words are abandoned in favor of highly personalized speech, which appears disjointed and meaningless to others ("word salad"). New words, *neologisms,* are coined to express private meanings. These bizarre thoughts (characteristic of the primary process) reflect unsuccessful attempts to cope with the pressures of underlying mental forces.

Other pathological manifestations of unconscious influence are to be found in severe cases of forgetting, or *amnesia.* Minor, selective amnesias often occur in normal individuals after a traumatic event, such as an automobile accident or a deep personal tragedy. Most extreme is the *fugue state,* in which a person attempts to escape from an unbearable situation by forgetting everything about himself and literally running away to another location. He no longer knows who he is and frequently wanders about in a dazed condition until apprehended for some reason, usually in connection with his peculiar behavior. Riding freight trains as a vagrant is a typical activity for this kind of amnesia victim. A rarer symptom with massive amnesia is *multiple personality,* a dissociative reaction in which the individual resolves a conflict by splitting the personality into two or more selves—each representing a different facet and totally unaware, at the conscious level, of the others' existence (see Thigpen, Thigpen, and Cleckley, 1957).

Everyday instances of forgetting motivated by unconscious forces belong to the category of *repression*, discussed on page 35. Freud (1938) gives detailed examples of mechanisms involved in the forgetting of names; terms from a foreign language; sequences of words; impressions; resolutions. Failure to remember the birthday of a close friend or relative, or "unintentionally" missing an appointment are common manifestations of the tendency to forget events somehow linked with anxiety, often stemming from unconscious hostility. In Freud's view, such omissions serve to "avoid the awakening of pain" which would accompany the thought's entry into consciousness. It should be pointed out that the conscious unpleasantness of an idea is not responsible for its being forgotten, but rather its unconscious connection with anxiety. Seemingly innocuous thoughts may themselves be repressed because of an indirect link of this sort. It follows that experiments which seek to test the concept of repression by utilizing materials rated consciously by subjects as "pleasant" or "unpleasant" are missing the mark.

A special phenomenon to which psychonanalysis has called attention is the *screen memory*, a derivative of the repressed idea, which enters consciousness as a substitute. It is as if the ego searches its store of memories to find an inoffensive replacement or screen for the unacceptable impulse pushing for discharge. Disturbing childhood events are typically supplanted by screen memories of surprising vividness and persistence.

THE ASSOCIATION OF IDEAS

Freud described the association of ideas as an unobstructed flow of energy from one memory trace to another. Ideas become connected initially through some similarity in content or simply by having occurred contiguously in time—that is, adjoining one another in sequence. Unconscious associations formed in the id are not so easily understood, since they obey the laws of primary-process thinking. To bring these unconscious determinants of thought to the surface, Freud devised the technique of *free association*. Patients in psychoanalytic treatment are required to obey the "fundamental rule" of saying whatever comes into mind without censoring it, no matter how irrelevant, painful, or senseless it seems at the moment. The chain of associations, allowed to unfold in this manner, often leads to the recovery of repressed or forgotten material underlying current symptoms and problem areas in the personality.[3] An uninterrupted flow of ideas is facilitated by having the patient

---

[3] Jung (1918) did research using a more *controlled* association method in which both normal and psychiatric subjects were verbally presented a series of stimulus words and instructed to respond to each with the first word that came to mind. Long reaction times and large galvanic skin responses, among other signs, were considered to indicate underlying mental *complexes*.

lie comfortably on a couch with the psychoanalyst seated unobtrusively nearby. Pauses or breaks in the chain assume significance as silent indicators of unconscious conflict *(resistance)* and further probing is then carried out.

Associative thinking, relatively undirected and uncontrolled, also characterizes *daydreaming*. One thought acts as a stimulus to another without concern for reality or meaningful organization. Serving as a type of wish fulfillment, the daydream obeys the pleasure principle in granting limited expression to sexual and aggressive urges. In other words, thought processes, during daydreaming, tend to be dominated by the id. An exploratory investigation of daydreaming in female college students showed that a boring task led to positively toned fantasies—exciting, pleasant, and ending happily (Bordin, 1964). In contrast to a condition of relaxation, anxiety over a possible electric shock tended to reduce the amount and intensity of visual imagery and curtailed the use of color in subsequent daydreams. The subject herself appeared as the main character more often in the anxiety condition and was described as "nervous," which seems to support the view that daydreams can function to lessen unpleasant tension by permitting its expression in fantasy.

DREAMS

The form of thought which has been studied most intensively from the standpoint of unconscious mental processes is, of course, the dream. As mentioned in Chapter 1, Freud conceived of the dream as "the royal road to the unconscious," and his book *The Interpretation of Dreams* (1900) provided major impetus to the psychoanalytic movement. A fair amount of dream content stems from events of the day *(day residues)*, thoughts prior to falling asleep, or even sounds heard while sleeping. Simple association links one idea to the next. But Freud made the insightful discovery that more complicated forces are also at work. Dreams were shown to represent, in disguised fashion, the wish-fulfilling expression of unconscious, unacceptable thoughts. Thus he drew the important distinction between *manifest*, or actual, content and the underlying *latent* meaning of the dream. Even anxiety-filled dreams are said to serve an adaptive function, since they reduce inner tension by permitting limited discharge of the anxiety.

One of the unconscious mechanisms by which "dream work" is accomplished is *condensation*. Through condensation, objectionable thoughts are disguised by being broken into elements and formed into new obscure combinations, resulting in such phenomena as mixed images or composite persons bearing the features of several different individuals. Freud (1938, p. 331) gives a personal illustration of dream condensation of words in the following passage:

A colleague sent an essay of his, in which he had, in my opinion, overestimated the value of a recent physiological discovery, and had expressed himself, moreover, in extravagant terms. On the following night I dreamed a sentence which obviously referred to this essay: "That is a truly norekdal style." The solution of this word-formation at first gave me some difficulty; it was unquestionably formed as a parody of the superlatives "colossal," "pyramidal"; but it was not easy to say where it came from. At last the monster fell apart into the two names *Nora* and *Ekdal*, from two well-known plays by Ibsen. I had previously read a newspaper article on Ibsen by the writer whose latest work I was now criticizing in my dream.

Another unconscious mechanism is *displacement,* by which the manifest content of the dream is purposely centered elsewhere than upon the essential aspects. For example, in analyzing his dream of having written a botanical monograph on a certain plant, Freud was able to trace many subtle connections to complex interpersonal relationships with his colleagues—the contrived monograph serving merely as an object upon which his troublesome unconscious attitudes could conveniently be displaced.

Symbolism is an especially frequent tool of the dream work. The symbol is an indirect representation which stands for something else, thereby contributing to the disguise of unacceptable impulses. The process is facilitated by the fact that thoughts are typically translated into pictorial images in dreams. Various principles of association—such as physical resemblance (size, shape, color, etc.), similar function, part-whole relationships, contrast, and occurrence together in time—lend themselves to the substitutive disguise. Certain associations are very common and reveal themselves over and over in dreams experienced by different people (though it is questionable whether—as Freud and Jung contend—some symbols appear universally among cultures). Common father symbols (teachers, judges, heads of government) have their origin in that all represent some form of authority; fire often symbolizes sexual passion, snakes represent the penis; the color yellow stands for urine; and so on.

Finally, there is the mechanism of *secondary elaboration,* by which the dream content is given an aura of coherence and intelligibility. Somehow an attempt is made unconsciously by the ego to connect the condensed, displaced, and symbolic parts of the dream (primary process) in a manner at least somewhat consistent with conscious logic. In other words, the ego's more advanced secondary-process thinking is not completely suspended during dream formation. But this pulling together of a senseless mass of thought fragments is mainly illusory from a logical standpoint and, the underlying emotional tone of the basic impulses remains unchanged.

The operation of dream mechanisms can be illustrated very simply by the productions of a hypnotized subject told to dream, on three different occasions, of "a square with a circle inside" (Blum, 1961, p. 175). The first dream was not preceded by any special instructions; the second came at the peak of an induced anxiety mood; and the third was in conjunction with a very happy mood. His hynotic reports immediately after each dream are given below:

1. (*no special instruction*) The square started turning slowly and kept going faster and faster and then it looked like a circle.
2. (*anxiety mood*) It was turned into a hammer or something and it kept coming toward me as if it were going to hit me. It never did—it would get close and then stop and then go away . . . come back at me again and keep getting closer and closer. And it kept doing that over and over again.
3. (*happy mood*) The circle came out of the square and seemed to be moving around the square in one direction and then it would stop and the square would start moving around the circle in the opposite direction and that was repeated over and over again. (Told with gestures as though describing a dance routine.)

Dream 1 represents an imaginal condensation—the square and circle literally lose their individual identity as the former merges into the latter. In Dream 2 displacement away from the original source of anxiety (the hypnotic mood induction) and symbolic translation of the frightening situation into a hammer are both evident. Dream 3, bizarre and illogical on the surface, illustrates a mental response, within the limits imposed by the task, to the stimulus of pleasure. The subject apparently associated dancing with a joyful mood, and the content may even have been influenced by associated thoughts of "square dancing" and "forming a circle."

Until several years ago the scientific study of dreams belonged almost exclusively to the psychoanalytic domain. With the advent of new experimental techniques, however, laboratory investigations have come into prominence (Dement and Kleitman, 1957). The discovery that dreaming is accompanied by rapid eye movements (REMs), recorded electrically with the eyelids closed, made it possible for experimenters to awaken subjects from periods of light sleep (when dreams typically occur) and obtain their immediate reports of what had just transpired. Many interesting facts about dreams in general have emerged from studies of this kind. For example, almost all subjects dream every night, with dreaming occupying about 20 per cent of sleeping time; the dream events do not happen in a flash as commonly believed; and the presence of color in dreams is very rare. A finding of potential dynamic significance is that persons awakened when they start to dream tend to make up for the loss by dreaming more on subsequent nights (Dement, 1960). This effect of "dream deprivation" indirectly supports Freud's belief that dreams serve a necessary function in the personality.

A recent survey (Foulkes, 1964) indicates that the thought content reported by subjects when awakened during a period of rapid eye movement is much more disguised, bizarre, and dramatic than thoughts elicited from awakenings in prior non-REM periods. The active processes of distortion during the dream phase tend to corroborate Freud's description of condensation, displacement, and symbolism. The pre-REM periods, on the other hand, seem to reflect the day residues—undisguised memories or re-creations of recent events in the dreamer's life which later get elaborated and woven into the dream fabric. This transition seems to contradict Freud's assertion that the dream appears from unconsciousness suddenly "like a firework, which takes hours to prepare but goes off in a moment."

Experimental investigation of day residues dates back to 1917 (Poetzl), when it was demonstrated that manifest content of dreams can be influenced by very brief exposures of "unnoticed" stimuli. Subjects were first shown landscapes for about 1/100 second and then asked to describe and draw what they had seen. Told subsequently to take note of any dreams that night, they returned the next day and narrated dream content related to aspects of the landscapes which had not even been reported in the previous session. Numerous replications and extensions of this phenomenon have been carried out in recent years (e.g., Fisher and Paul, 1959; Luborsky and Shevrin, 1956).

COGNITIVE CONTROLS

A group of psychologists working within a general psychoanalytic framework has evolved the concept of *cognitive controls*—enduring response dispositions which regulate the impact of environmental pressures and inner impulses (Gardner et al., 1959). These individual consistencies in organizing cognitive behavior are integrally related to the ego-psychology point of view described earlier (see p. 19), since the controls reflect the unconscious operation of ego structures in adapting to the various external and internal forces. Emerging in the course of development and shaped by both constitutional and experiential factors, controls tend to be invariant, for a given individual, over broad ranges of laboratory tasks and environmental conditions. The particular pattern of an individual's set of controls is referred to as his *cognitive style*.

Among the first controls to be elaborated and studied was *leveling-sharpening*, interpreted as the blurring versus heightening of fine distinctions among a set of stimuli presented in sequence. "Levelers" were hypothesized to suffer from a deficiency of available attention, which limits their capacity for concentration. A link to the defense mechanism of repression was made from research indicating that persons whose memory organizations fall in the leveling category tend to cope with internal conflicts by repression. Leveling was presumed to be a "necessary but insufficient" precondition for the occurrence of repression.

Two cognitive control principles which have been singled out recently (Silverman, 1964) for their special relevance to the problem of attention, particularly with reference to schizophrenia, are scanning and field articulation. *Scanning* pertains to differences among individuals in regard to the extensiveness with which stimuli are sampled. Those who scan a great deal, looking back and forth repeatedly from one segment of the visual field to another (as judged from films of eye movements), tend, for example, to be more accurate in estimating the size of a standard stimulus, whereas limited scanners generally overestimate size. Schizophrenics fall at the extremes of either marked or minimal scanning in contrast to normal groups, who typically are in the moderate range. Extensive scanning has also been linked to the defenses of isolation and projection.

Field articulation describes differences in attention to certain segments of complex stimulus fields and simultaneous inhibition of attention to other segments. In other words, attention can be mobilized in greater or lesser degree upon the most relevant aspects. The selectivity with which paranoid schizophrenics concentrate on particular persons and specific situations to build their highly systematized, delusional complex of ideas is ascribed to overuse of the field-articulation principle of cognitive control.

PROBLEM SOLVING

The view that unconscious mental processes can play a significant role in creative problem solving has been illustrated in numerous anecdotes. A favorite is the quotation cited at the beginning of this chapter. The formulation of the benzene ring theory by Kekule in 1865 proved vital to the development of the science of organic chemistry. Whatever the reasons behind the appearance of snakes in his dream, the fact remains that his previous waking thoughts on the problem of the arrangement of carbon and hydrogen somehow combined with the visual imagery of the dream to suggest the solution.

The famous French mathematician, Henri Poincaré (1956), has written of the manner in which he achieved various notable insights in his work:

. . . One evening contrary to my custom, I drank black coffee and could not sleep. Ideas rose in crowds; I felt them collide until pairs interlocked, so to speak, making a stable combination. By the next morning

I had established the existence of a class of Fuchsian functions, those which come from the hypergeometric series; I had only to write out the results, which took but a few hours.

. . . The changes of travel made me forget my mathematical work. Having reached Coutances, we entered an omnibus to go someplace or other. At the moment when I put my foot on the step the idea came to me, without anything in my former thoughts seeming to have paved the way for it, that the transformations I had used to define the Fuchsian functions were identical with those of non-Euclidean geometry. I did not verify the idea: I should not have had time, as, upon taking my seat in the omnibus, I went on with a conversation already commenced, but I felt a perfect certainty. On my return to Caen, for conscience' sake I verified the result at my leisure.

Most striking at first is this appearance of sudden illumination, a manifest sign of long, unconscious prior work. The role of this unconscious work in mathematical invention appears to me incontestable, and traces of it would be found in other cases where it is less evident (pp. 2044–2045).

He remarks further that a rest period during a concerted attack on a problem not only gives the mind back its force and freshness but also allows the "unconscious work" to continue uninterrupted. Emotional aspects of these unconscious mental activities are especially important, for they play a part in determining which ones emerge into conscious awareness. According to Poincaré, those ideas which survive the filtering process appeal to a "special esthetic sensibility" of beauty, harmony, and elegance.

The psychoanalyst Ernst Kris (1950) contrasts the dynamics of fantasy and problem solving. In fantasy, freely wandering thought processes tend to discharge more libido and aggression and less neutralized energy than in problem solving. The ego's processes are largely in the service of the id and the pleasure principle. In problem solving, on the other hand, the autonomous ego interests take over, employing neutralized ego energy and keeping sexual and aggressive discharges to a minimum (see p. 19). With respect to creative thinking, he distinguishes between the inspirational and elaborational phases. During the period of inspiration the ego permits a certain amount of controlled regression by withdrawing some of its countercathectic energies. This *regression in the service of the ego* facilitates the emergence of primary-process material at the preconscious level, making potentially original ideas more accessible to consciousness than otherwise. Through subsequent elaboration which proceeds slowly, the secondary process evaluates these inspirations in the context of reality—discarding those which are obviously bizarre and carefully working over the ones which show promise of meeting the test of public acceptance.

INFLUENCES UPON ACTION

PATHOLOGICAL EFFECTS

The way unconscious mental forces influence action parallels the way they affect perception and thought. Some of the most serious and extensive impairments of muscle function occur in *catatonia,* a severe form of schizophrenia. Deeply regressed patients suffering from this disorder typically show two symptoms—*catalepsy* and *bizarre movements.* The former, involving extreme muscular rigidity, is attributed to the inhibition of unacceptable, unconscious impulses to act—e.g., a desire to strike someone. These pent-up impulses create strong muscle tensions which, not being discharged, maintain the rigidity. Some bizarre movements, such as "meaningless" smiles, are considered to be vestiges or remains of previous action tendencies. Smiling in a "disarming," friendly fashion, originally serving the defensive function of warding off potentially threatening behavior by other individuals, gradually degenerates in the course of the disease to an inappropriate expression. Some bizarre acts may represent unsuccessful attempts to regain contact with reality, an illustration being unconscious imitation of the gestures of persons in the environment.

Hysterical paralysis, capable of involving almost any part of the body, is analogous to the functional blindness discussed earlier. Conversion symptoms (see p. 49), such as a paralyzed hand, symbolize unconscious conflicts. The absence of a purely physical basis for the disability is revealed by the fact that the afflicted area often does not correspond to what would be expected from the pattern of nerve and muscle distribution in that area. A paralysis affecting one half of the body may not overlap the midline, as an organic disease typically does. Additional inconsistencies are revealed when the limb can be made to function in certain situations—under hypnosis, for example—but never in others. Motor paralyses in general serve as unconscious defenses against action. An illustration is *hysterical mutism,* the inability to speak, which may represent hostility or anxiety over sexual temptations experienced toward persons in whose presence the symptom develops. The struggle between opposing impulses can create an increase in muscular tonus leading to rigidity and loss of function. Though consciously unpleasant and disabling, the symptom nevertheless is a compromise, preventing the eruption of even more traumatic repressed desires.

Lack of an initial organic cause in no way minimizes the seriousness of these afflictions. The involved muscle can waste away through disuse, and the impairment may become irreversible over a period of time. The particular part of the body affected in a given "psychosomatic" case depends upon a combination of factors, including constitutional weakness already existing in an organ; the situation in which the organ is most active and under the greatest tension; and the ability of that organ to express the unconscious force symbolically (e.g., oral incorporative tendencies can best be expressed via the mouth; anal ones are linked readily to the intestinal tract).

A less severe manifestation is the *psychogenic tic*, an automatic movement in the voluntary muscular system which occurs independently of the person's will. This category encompasses the large variety of repetitive nervous mannerisms—meaningless movements, twitches, and the like. These useless acts, also conversion symptoms, presumably have their origin in highly emotional, repressed situations and can symbolize many different functions, such as movements of rage, masturbatory gestures, or reassurance against fear. The striving for discharge of the unconscious force is said to conflict with an opposing tendency, which eventually results in an accumulation of energy released abortively and involuntarily in a kind of neural short-circuiting. *Tremors* and *spasms* or cramps, without real organic involvement, are similarly classed as conversion reactions.

A common phenomenon in which movements are directly controlled by unconscious mental forces is *sleepwalking*. The somnambulist moves about with eyes open while apparently still asleep, and typically is unable to remember afterward what happened. More prevalent among children, the symptom indicates a blurring of the distinction between sleep and waking life. Dynamically, the actions in this dissociative state often carry out unconscious wishes inherent in the latent meaning of accompanying dreams. In the ordinary waking state the same wish would not be permitted translation into overt behavior. Sometimes the particular movements may be more intimately related to the manifest dream content —for example, the sleeping child who walks into his parents' bedroom, not because of an unconscious voyeuristic tendency, but rather to seek reassurance against a frightening episode in his dream. Occasionally the sleepwalking may represent nothing more than a general condition of restlessness due to internal tensions.

Chronic fatigue is a neurotic symptom not specific to a given conflict but rather reflecting the generally large investment of countercathectic energy in opposing the breakthrough of impulses. Persons in conflict tend to become tired more quickly. The physical effect is ascribed to the abnormal muscular tensions in individuals undergoing pervasive mental stress. The exact nature of these physiological processes is not known, but it is assumed that the chemical alterations responsible for fatigue (e.g., increase of lactic acid in the muscles and lowering of blood sugar) are induced by changes in muscular behavior.

A specific neurotic symptom bearing on action is *compulsion*, closely related to obsession (discussed on page 53). In fact, the two are linked in the psychiatric classification "obsessive-compulsive reaction." Just as an obsession is a persistent, recurring thought, a compulsion is experienced as an irresistible impulse to carry out some act. The ego, in order to avert being overwhelmed by anxiety, has to obey strange inner commands which contradict its own judgment. A handwashing compulsion, for example, serves the defensive function of helping to ward off a threatening superego concerned over "dirty" thoughts. Also akin to compulsions are *phobias*, in which anxiety over internal conflicts is projected into fears of external objects or situations, which must be avoided at all costs. Fears of high places, crowded rooms, or open spaces are familiar illustrations. *Counterphobic* attitudes in which some persons paradoxically show a preference for the very situations they fear, represent overcompensations for anxiety.

SLIPS

The influence of unconscious mental forces upon action is by no means confined to the realm of pathology. Emotional disturbances clearly can interfere with muscle functions, so that a normal person may become weak at a time of crisis or even "paralyzed" by extreme fear. Perhaps the most common manifestations are slips of the tongue or pen. Temporary failure of repression can result in the sudden, "unintentional" appearance of an underlying thought which would ordinarily be kept down. Actually the error represents a form of compromise, since the impulse gains some measure of expression in consciousness yet does not emerge intact. It is easily dismissed as a simple mistake.

Freud (1943) cites the example of the impatient and disgruntled president, who opened a session of his parliament with the words "Gentlemen, I declare a quorum present and herewith declare the session *closed.*" Freud illustrated a slip of the pen with the case of a murderer, who had obtained highly dangerous disease germs from scientific institutions by posing as a bacteriologist. Once he complained to the authorities of one of these institutions about the ineffectiveness of the cultures sent him and, instead of the words "in my experiments on mice and guinea pigs" (in German, "Mausen und Meerschweinchen"), wrote "in my experiments on people" ("Menschen").

A large proportion of such mistakes are considered by Freud to have dynamic significance. He extends this deterministic view even further in maintaining generally, apart from simple slips, that behavior is often *overdetermined.* A single act may serve simultaneously to reduce pressures created by a variety of unconscious forces. For example, behavior fulfilling a demand of the external world may at the same time gratify an impulse and also satisfy the superego. Ego psychologists have incorporated this notion in the principle of *multiple function,* which holds that the organism has a tendency to achieve maximum effect with minimum effort.

BOREDOM

The experience of boredom, often accompanied by restlessness and a desire to "do something else," has been linked to unconscious forces. The major psychonanalytic writer on this topic was Fenichel (1951), who drew a distinction between "pathological" and "normal" types of boredom. In the former an unacceptable drive or desire is not permitted access to consciousness in order to prevent anxiety. More specifically, the aim of the drive (see p. 3) is repressed, but the tension remains. The blocked discharge leads to feelings of unpleasantness and constraint. In the normal type of boredom, the expected discharge is thwarted, not via intrapsychic conflict but by external pressures in the real world. The constraint felt by a student trapped in his seat during an exceedingly dull lecture need not be elaborated.

A few psychologists also have theorized about the nature of boredom. Hebb (1958) pointed to the role of prolonged repetition of environmental stimuli in creating an aversive state of low arousal. In order to dispel the unpleasantness of this state, the organism actively searches for new stimulation containing sufficient variety to raise arousal to a moderate level. Berlyne (1960) speculated about the physiological mechanisms involved in boredom: monotonous input dulls or inhibits the cerebral cortex, which then loses its control over the reticular system in the midbrain; the latter "flares" up and increases arousal; finally novel, surprising, uncertain, or complex stimuli restore cortical control and arousal decreases.

Recently Geiwitz (1964) carried out an empirical study of the structure of boredom. He investigated the role of four factors—mental arousal, constraint, unpleasantness, and repetitiveness—by hypnotically controlled experiments. The four college students who served as subjects were first trained extensively to become reliable reporters of their own degrees of boredom, beginning with the reliving under hypnosis of boring classroom experiences from their past. Independent verification of the reports was accomplished by ratings of overt behavior along a scale ranging from "very withdrawn, weary" to "fairly alert and responsive"; and also by the amount of deterioration (carelessness, sloppiness) in the simple routine task of placing check marks in a series of boxes.

The analysis and synthesis of boredom was then attempted in several phases of experimentation. Analysis took the form of assessing the degree of each of the four factors, plus level of boredom, at the conclusion of varying durations of the repetitive task. The results showed strong relationships of boredom to low mental arousal, high constraint, high unpleasantness, and increased feelings of repetitiveness. The synthesis of boredom was approached by inducing each of the four factors posthypnotically in specified degrees. Here the data indicated that low mental arousal and high constraint each produced boredom with the other three factors held constant; the effects of unpleasantness and repetitiveness alone were much less clear.

A CASE STUDY OF DISTURBED VISUAL IMAGERY [4]

Since Chapters 1 and 2 deal primarily with concepts, research illustrations have been given in the last section of each. The present chapter already has cited numerous empirical investigations in the context of unconscious influences upon perceiving, thinking, and acting. Therefore a more useful addition at this point may be the detailed account of an unexpected episode involving a subject in our laboratory some years ago. The dynamics of a disturbance in visual imagery are vividly illustrated. It began when the experimenter (E) queried the subject (S) under hypnosis as follows:

E: Sleep more and more deeply now as we talk. I'd like to talk to you about colors and what meaning they have for you. I've noticed several times that colors have been important in things that you see while you're asleep here and colors are also important in your responses to words.

S: Yes. They seem to be present always every time I think of something. There are usually colors I see first and then the colors take the form of something.

E: When you're awake as well as when you're asleep?

S: Yes. It's just that when something is said, or I see something, or I'm asked to reply to something, a color or a series of colors will flash into my mind. Then, after concentrating on these colors, they take a form or a shape or spell out a word, and then this is what my reply comes from.

E: And this is true of all the thoughts you have while you're awake?

S: Yes.

E: Is it happening now as we talk?

S: Yes.

E: Tell me what colors are going through your mind now as we're talking.

S: Several shades of green and orange and a large block sort of between a red and a purple.

E: Is this distracting to you when you see these colors?

S: No, it's never distracting. It's very normal—or at least I never thought of it as being distracting. It always has been there.

E: When was the youngest period of your life that you remember having this?

S: As far as I know I've always remembered it. I could always picture things in color and remember things that were taking place. They always took the form of colors and then I could see what it was. It wasn't until high school that I was able to make the colors form words or letters.

[4] Abridged from Chapter 14 of *A Model of the Mind* (Blum, 1961).

When I was asked to spell something I always spelled directly from the color to the word without seeing the letters or how the word was put together.

E: This happened in high school? Give me an example of what you're talking about.

S: It was the eleventh grade. I had an English instructor who was very much disturbed by the fact that I couldn't spell. So she asked me what came into my mind when she asked me to spell a word. She picked out a very simple word—RAN—and immediately red, darker red, and brown flashed into my mind and that stood for the RAN. The R was red, the deeper red became the A, and then the N turned to a brown, so there's a band of color that flashed through my mind. It was a continuum . . . She told me I should concentrate on making the color become the letter that it was supposed to represent and so I was trying to concentrate on that for a while. I could see the letter in the color that I had previously just seen the color.

E: After you learned to do this did the same color stand for the same letter?

S: The colors were basically the same, in other words all Rs were basically red, but the shade of red changed depending upon how the word was used or how the letter was used in the word. For example, in a word like RATHER the R in RA would tend to be more toward the purple, and in the ER the E is green and the R very definitely red . . .

E: Are there other mental events that don't have the colors?

S: Whenever I'm asked a question and I don't know the answer, my mind turns black and white or gray and I see nothing . . . just free forms . . . sort of like a haze, looking through a cloud, and nothing comes to mind. Only when color enters into it do I think of something to say. When I am asked a question like those that you ask, there are just patches of color, many different colors, and they flash by in my mind very rapidly. Then one stops and becomes more stabilized . . . and when I concentrate on that one the color takes a form, either facts or people moving or things happening, and it becomes very vivid, just as I have seen them before . . .

E: Colors have connotations for most people—there are warm colors, soft colors—I wonder if you could tell me what connotations, what feelings various colors have for you?

S: There doesn't seem to be any particular emotional effect if a color is flashed. It doesn't necessarily make me feel a certain way. Light green and yellows do give me a feeling of the outdoors and enable me to see pictures of being outdoors and feel as though I'm right there, but red doesn't seem to take either side. A little toward the purple, red could be very violent or it could be very depressing. When it's toward the yellow, it could be more gay and free. It can be many different things.

E: How about other colors?

S: Green more or less is always very pleasant—when it's very yellowish it becomes very bright sunlight and when it becomes deeper it's more like the shadows in a very dense forest. Bluish green feels like all outdoors—the sea, the trees, the sky—and becomes a very wonderful warm feeling.

Blue is another color that's quite a bit like green, except royal blue has sort of a synthetic quality, never looks real. If it's a light blue it's more like the sky, and if it's a very dark blue it begins to take the form or the feeling of black or very deep and morbid colors. Brown is another color that I see very frequently and again it has a lot of mixed feelings depending upon what it's with. It can be very gay or very depressing. Sometimes when something is said that makes me very mad, everything I see is brown. Yet other times when something is very happy, I'll see brown and yellow and green all together.

E: How do you see the colors when they're all together?

S: They're not any definite form at first . . . the colors may be whirling in a sort of funnel form or they're unusual free forms that have no definite meaning. When the moving patch of colors stops, then I can concentrate on it and make a face out of it or a person or some other object related to the color I was thinking about. Before it's more like a mist constantly changing, sort of like a steam bath where the steam is moving and changing shape.

Next an attempt was made to track down the genesis of the colors by having S "relive" under hypnosis episodes from his early life. The following was one of his recollections at age three or four:

S: I see my father as he goes to the front door and leaves in the morning. I've either just gotten up or I'm usually sitting in the living room in my pajamas. He leaves and that's all I see of him until the next morning at the same time. He's very irritated, very grouchy, and I'm afraid of him. I don't dare say anything to him.

E: What do you think as you're sitting there in your pajamas? What thought crosses your mind?

S: I'm thinking why don't I stay in the bedroom until he leaves and then I don't ever have to see him.

E: And is this thought in picture form?

S: I just picture the fact that I stayed in the bedroom—in my bed or else I can stand around and look out the window or be getting dressed. I can hear my father stomp out of the house and then I can go out in the living room and he's gone, and everything is left to me and my mother.

His mother appeared in quite another context:

E: Continue to sleep very, very deeply and now let's go back to a time when you were even younger. Let's go back to the first house you lived in. Tell me where you are and what's happening now.

S: It's late in the night and I'm sleeping on a mattress on the floor. I'm not quite three years old. I feel I have to go to the bathroom but I don't know to get up out of bed and go into the bathroom. I start urinating, or I've been urinating ever since I've been thinking that I have to go to the bathroom. And as I'm urinating I can see in my mind that on the bedsheet will be a large yellow rose. And I think to myself how pleased my mother will be to have this large yellow rose. And then I drift back to sleep.

E: Now, as you're still at this age in the same place, tell me what thoughts flash through your mind as I say "yellow."

S: I see this large yellow rose.

E: Now think of your father and tell me what thoughts go through your mind.

S: When I think of my father the color brown comes to mind.

E: What picture does it change into?

S: There is no picture. In fact I can't even picture my father. It's a very dark and gloomy brown, sort of a grayish brown. Everything seems to be brown . . . there's no shape or form, it's just like a mist and everything is brown in color.

E: All right, tell me now what colors come to mind as I mention different people. Remember you're still less than three years old. *Mother* . . .

S: When you mentioned mother, I could see my mother with a large yellow rose. It was bigger than she was or almost as big as she was. She could hold it in her hands. And I was lying on the couch—on the mattress rather—and she was saying how beautiful it was and how much she loved it, and I was so wonderful to give it to her.

Later on the relationship between father and brown was elaborated:

E: All right, tell me what comes to mind when I say *Father?*

S: Brown.

E: Tell me more about it.

S: When you mentioned father, the colors that were whirling around in my mind suddenly disappeared and everything turned brown in color. Then the word "father" was printed out in lower case letters across this brown background, and in the loop part of the "f" appeared my father's face. Then as the word "father" disappeared my father stood there all in the same colors of brown . . .

E: Now think of your father in two or three different situations and describe the colors.

S: Well, one that comes to mind is right after he had been fishing or hunting. He wears the same light brown sort of a tan coat and pair of trousers . . . and more of a yellowish brown hat . . . and his face is darker brown because of his whiskers and being tan from the sun . . . and he has a brown tackle box or brown case that his gun is in.

E: Now think of your father in another setting and tell me about it.

S: I see him in a brown topcoat, brown hat, brown suit. He's leaving for work. He just puts his coat on and walks out the door.

E: Now let's take a third setting.

S: I can see him out in the yard working in his garden. This time he has on gray clothes—gray trousers and a brown plaid shirt, but it's more gray than brown. He's digging in the ground, which is a dark brown. There's peat moss around which is a reddish brown. The shovel he's using is a rusty color . . .

E: What feeling does the color brown have for you? What is your emotional reaction when you see it?

S: It makes me feel as though it's drab, something I wouldn't want to wear.

E: Anything else?

S: I always associate it with bowel movement.

E: When did you first make that association?

S: I recall that when I was quite young, about ten, I was playing with some clay. It was right after Christmas and my sister had gotten a set of oil base clays which we could make things out of. I had the brown piece and I was wadding it up in my hand and squeezing it. When I let go of it I noticed how it looked so much like a bowel movement, and I said something about it. Everyone yelled at me so I stopped and made something out of the clay instead.

E: All right, let's go back to your father and the color brown. You know the connotation that brown has—this is the connotation that brown tends to have for all children—it means feces. And feces are very important in the life of a young child. He has to learn to be toilet trained and sometimes parents get very concerned about this, so it becomes a central conflict between parents and children. The children are often frustrated and one of the ways they get back is through fantasies involving smearing. Does that make sense to you?

S: It seems to be very logical that this is the way a child would fight back against something.

E: So if you were mad at your father and couldn't fight back in any other way, you would fight back in your imagination.

S: Yes.

E: So you have some understanding of what might have been the relationship between the color brown and your father.

S: Yes.

The connection between mother and yellow also was amplified:

S: I always see my mother as being yellow.

E: And yellow is gay and happy, or not?

S: Mostly it is but not all the time.

E: Do you remember what you said last time that related yellow to mother?

S: Yes. You mentioned my mother twice. The first time I saw a very light and very gay yellow rose, and then afterwards I saw a very drab, sort of a brownish yellowish green color and exactly the opposite feeling.

E: Where did the yellow rose come from?

S: That was the yellow rose that was formed by my urine.

E: You said that the yellow rose was a present you had given to your mother. Why would a child have this kind of a fantasy—when he wets the bed, thinking that this is a present he's giving to his mother?

S: He would think that it was part of him . . . he's giving to his mother a part of himself.

E: All right, now we have some understanding of what meaning the association of yellow with your mother might have, don't we?

S: Yes.

Subsequently, these dynamic links between father-brown and mother-yellow were utilized in a modified form of hypnotherapy to rid the subject of his color symptoms, which he believed to impair his ability to read, write, and spell—a successful resolution of the strange case of the "yellow rose cathexis."

CONCLUSION

This small volume has sought to define and treat the content of psychodynamics in such a way as to bring it more into the mainstream of the academic discipline of psychology. In Chapter 1, unconscious mental forces were outlined and then traced in their effects through the developmental stages from infancy to adulthood. The dominant views of Freud in this regard were supplemented by the positions of the early deviants from the psychoanalytic fold—Adler, Jung, and Rank; the neo-Freudian school; and the "ego" psychologists. Chapter 2 concentrated on the topic of anxiety and its unconsciously produced reactions. Anxiety was examined from the standpoint of its nature, origins, identification, and functions. Reactions included the series of defense mechanisms as well as a variety of other behavioral responses. Finally, in Chapter 3, unconscious influences were related directly to the major concerns of psychology—perceiving, thinking, and acting. The range of unconscious mental forces in creating abnormal manifestations and also in shaping normal behavior was explored in some detail for each process in turn.

Research illustrations attesting to the verifiability of psychodynamic assertions were interspersed throughout in a further effort to integrate the material more fully with traditional academic psychology. It was demonstrated that a variety of approaches can be brought to bear upon seemingly elusive issues which can be examined by conventional research methods—e.g., controlled observations, ratings, and experimental situations; modified projective techniques like the Blacky Pictures; and hypnotically controlled laboratory studies. It is hoped that these examples will help to end the storm of controversy over the scientific respectability of dynamic hypotheses.

The foregoing should not be misinterpreted as a glowing endorsement of the present level of knowledge in the area. As mentioned at the very outset, psychodynamic theory is not in a highly developed state. Neither orthodox psychoanalysis nor its variants now provide a tight, well-knit body of concepts from which systematic empirical studies logically emerge, although Rapaport (1959) has made a noteworthy attempt to clarify and elaborate Freudian formulations. The writer's own bias leads in the direction of designing new theoretical models rather than attempting to pull together the many loose threads in existing ones. Specifically, a program of research has evolved from a systems approach which seeks to spell out in more detail the cognitive processes intervening between stimulus and response (Blum, 1961, 1963). But apart from the form taken by any alternative conceptual scheme, one fact remains abundantly clear: The ultimate theory of the human mind will have to come to grips with the rich complexity of unconscious mental phenomena which Freud and his followers have so forcefully called to our attention.

REFERENCES

Adler, A. *A study of organ inferiority and its psychical compensation* (trans. S. E. Jelliffe). Nervous and Mental Disease Monograph Series, No. 24, New York, 1917.

——————. *Understanding human nature* (trans. W. B. Wolfe). New York: Greenberg, 1927.

Berlyne, D. E. *Conflict, arousal, and curiosity.* New York: McGraw-Hill, 1960.

Blum, G. S. A study of the psychoanalytic theory of psychosexual development. *Genet, Psychol. Monogr.*, 1949, 39, 3–99.

——————. *The Blacky Pictures: A technique for the exploration of personality dynamics.* Ann Arbor: Psychodynamic Instruments, 1950.

——————. *Psychoanalytic theories of personality.* New York: McGraw-Hill, 1953.

——————. An experimental reunion of psychoanalytic theory with perceptual vigilance and defense. *J. abn. soc. Psychol.*, 1954, 49, 94–98.

——————. Perceptual defense revisited. *J. abn. soc. Psychol.*, 1955, 51, 24–29.

——————. Defense preferences in four countries. *J. proj. Tech.*, 1956, 20, 33–41.

——————. An investigation of perceptual defense in Italy. *Psychol. Rep.*, 1957, 3, 169–175.

——————. *A model of the mind.* New York: Wiley, 1961.

——————. A guide for research use of the Blacky Pictures. *J. proj. Tech.*, 1962, 26, 3–29.

——————. Programming people to simulate machines. In S. S. Tomkins and S. J. Messick (Eds.), *Computer simulation of personality.* New York: Wiley, 1963.

——————. Defense preferences among university students in Denmark, France, Germany, and Israel. *J. proj. Tech.*, 1964, 28, 13–19.

——————, and Miller, D. R. Exploring the psychoanalytic theory of the "oral character." *J. Personal.*, 1952, 20, 287–304.

Bordin, Martha. The effects of relaxation, boredom, and anxiety upon daydreaming. Unpublished study, University of Michigan, 1964.

Boring, E. G. *A history of experimental psychology.* New York: Appleton-Century, 1929.

Clark, R. A. The projective measurement of experimentally induced sexual motivation. *J. exp. Psychol.*, 1952, 44, 391–399.

Cohen, A. R. Experimental effects of ego-defense preference on interpersonal relations. *J. abn. soc. Psychol.*, 1956, 52, 19–27.

Dement, W. The effect of dream deprivation. *Science*, 1960, 131, 1705–1707.

—————, and Kleitman, N. The relation of eye movements during sleep to dream activity: an objective method for the study of dreaming. *J. exp. Psychol.*, 1957, 53, 339–346.

Dollard, J., and Miller, N. E. *Personality and psychotherapy.* New York: McGraw-Hill, 1950.

Erikson, E. *Childhood and society.* New York: Norton, 1950.

Fechner, G. T. *Elemente der Psychophysik.* Leipzig: Breitkopf & Hartel, 1860.

Fenichel, O. *The psychoanalytic theory of neurosis.* New York: Norton, 1945.

—————. On the psychology of boredom. In D. Rapaport (Ed.), *Organization and pathology of thought.* New York: Columbia University Press, 1951, (pp. 349–361).

Findlay, A. *A hundred years of Chemistry* (3rd ed.). London: Duckworth, 1965.

Fisher, C., and Paul, I. H. The effect of subliminal visual stimulation on imagery and dreams: A validation study. *J. Amer. psychoanal. Assoc.*, 1959, 7, 35–83.

Foulkes, D. Theories of dream formation and recent studies of sleep consciousness. *Psychol. Bull.*, 1964, 62, 236–247.

Freud, Anna. *The ego and the mechanisms of defence* (trans. C. Baines). New York: Internat. Universities Press, 1946.

Freud, S. *The ego and the id.* Hogarth: London, 1927.

—————. *The problem of anxiety.* New York: Norton, 1936.

—————. The interpretation of dreams. In *The basic writings of Sigmund Freud.* (trans. and ed. by A. A. Brill). New York: Modern Library, 1938.

—————. The psychopathology of everyday life. In *The basic writings of Sigmund Freud* (trans. and ed. by A. A. Brill). New York: Modern Library, 1938.

—————. *A general introduction to psychoanalysis* (trans. Joan Riviere). New York: Garden City Publishing Co., 1943.

Fromm, E. *Escape from freedom.* New York: Farrar & Rinehart, 1941.

—————. *Man for himself.* New York: Rinehart, 1947.

Gardner, R. W., et al. Cognitive control: A study of individual consistencies in cognitive behavior. *Psychol. Issues*, 1959, 1, 1–185.

Geiwitz, P. J. *The structure of boredom.* Unpublished doctoral dissertation, University of Michigan, 1964.

Goldstein, K. *Human nature.* Cambridge: Harvard University Press, 1940.

Greenacre, Phyllis. The predisposition to anxiety. *Psychoanal. Quart.*, 1941, 10, 66–94, 610–638.

Hartmann, E. von. *Die Philosophie des Unbewussten,* 3 vols. Berlin, 1869.

Hartmann, H. Ego psychology and the problem of adaptation. In D. Rapaport (Ed.), *Organization and pathology of thought.* New York: Columbia University Press, 1951, 362–396.

——————, Kris, E., & Loewenstein, R. M. Comments on the formation of psychic structure. *Psychoanal. study of the child.* 1946, vol. 2, 11–38.

Hebb, D. O. *A textbook of psychology.* Philadelphia: Saunders, 1958.

Helmholtz, H. von. *Handbuch der physiologischen Optik.* Hamburg, Leipzig, 1866.

Herbart, J. F. *Lehrbuch zur Psychologie.* Koenigsberg, 1816.

Holzman, P. S. and Klein, G. S. Motive and style in reality contact. *Bull. Menninger Clin.,* 1956, *20,* 181–191.

Horney, Karen. *New ways in psychoanalysis.* New York: Norton, 1939.

——————. *Our inner conflicts.* New York: Norton, 1945.

Jenkin, N. Affective processes in perception. *Psychol. Bull.,* 1957, *54,* 100–127.

Jones, E. *The life and work of Sigmund Freud,* 3 vols. New York: Basic Books, 1953, 1956, 1957.

Jung, C. G. *Psychological types or the psychology of individuation* (trans. H. G. Baynes). New York: Harcourt, Brace, 1926.

——————. *The psychology of the unconscious* (trans. Beatrice M. Hinkle). New York: Dodd, Mead, 1927.

Kessen, W. and Mandler, G. Anxiety, pain, and the inhibition of distress. *Psychol. Rev.,* 1961, *68,* 396–404.

Krause, M. S. The measurement of transitory anxiety. *Psychol. Rev.,* 1961, *68,* 178–189.

Kris, E. On preconscious mental processes. *Psychoanal. Quart.,* 1950, *19,* 540–560.

Leibniz, G. W. von. *Monadologie,* 1714.

Luborsky, L. and Shevrin, H. Dreams and day residues: A study of the Poetzl observation. *Bull. Menninger Clinic,* 1956, *20,* 135–148.

MacKinnon, D. W. and Dukes, W. F. Repression. In L. Postman (Ed.), *Psychology in the making.* New York: Knopf, 1962. (pp. 662–744).

Martin, B. The assessment of anxiety by physiological behavioral measures. *Psychol. Bull.,* 1961, *58,* 234–255.

Mattson, J. M. and Natsoulas, T. Emotional arousal and stimulus duration as determinants of stimulus selection. *J. abn. soc. Psychol.,* 1962, *65,* 142–144.

May, R. *The meaning of anxiety.* New York: Ronald, 1950.

Nelson, S. E. Psychosexual conflicts and defenses in visual perception. *J. abn. soc. Psychol.,* 1955, *51,* 427–433.

Perloe, S. I.   Inhibition as a determinant of perceptual defense. *Perc. & Mot. Skills*, 1960, *11*, 59–66.

Poetzl, O.   Experimentell erregte Traumbilder in ihren Beziehungen zum indirekten Sehen. Z. *Neurol. Psychiat.*, 1917, *37*, 278–349.

Poincaré, H.   Mathematical creation. In J. R. Newman, (Ed.), *The world of mathematics*, Vol. IV, New York: Simon & Schuster, 1956.

Postman, L.   On the problem of perceptual defense. *Psychol. Rev.*, 1953, *60*, 298–306.

Rank, O.   *The trauma of birth.* New York: Harcourt, Brace, 1929.

Rapaport, D.   The structure of psychoanalytic theory: A systematizing attempt. In S. Koch, (Ed.), *Psychology: A study of a science.* New York: McGraw-Hill, 1959. (pp. 55–183).

Raush, H. L.   Perceptual constancy in schizophrenia: I. Size constancy. *J. Personal.*, 1952, *21*, 176–187.

Shellow, R. S.   *Perceptual distortion in the spatial localization of emotionally meaningful stimuli.* Unpublished doctoral dissertation, University of Michigan, 1956.

Silverman, J.   The problem of attention in research and theory in schizophrenia. *Psychol. Rev.*, 1964, *71*, 352–379.

Smock, C. D.   Replication and comments: "An experimental reunion of psychoanalytic theory with perceptual vigilance and defense." *J. abn. soc. psychol.*, 1956, *53*, 68–73.

Sullivan, H. S.   *The interpersonal theory of psychiatry.* New York: Norton, 1953.

Thigpen, C. H., Thigpen, H., and Cleckley, H. M.   *The three faces of Eve.* New York: McGraw-Hill, 1957.

Webster's New Collegiate Dictionary. Springfield: Merriam, 1960.

Weintraub, D. J. and Walker, E. L.   *Perception.* Belmont: Wadsworth, 1966.

Witkin, H. A., et al.   *Personality through perception.* New York: Harper, 1954.

INDEX